ALBERTO ALESSI

The Dream Factory

ALESSI SINCE 1921

Electa/Alessi

Overall Coordination
Renato Sartori, Marco Marabelli

Editors
Stefano Zuffi/Electa,
Oriana Cremella/Alessi, Agnese Piana/Alessi,
Daniela Zilocchi/Alessi

With the collaboration of
Gloria Barcellini, Ausilia Fortis,
Grazia Pagani

With thanks to
Lowe Lintas Pirella Göttsche,
Sottsass Associati, Studio Quadrifoglio,
Patrizia Scarzella,
Simona Oreglia, Sara Salvi,
Rossella Savio, Gabriella Cursoli

Cover Illustration
"The City of Towers,"
VIIIth International Exhibition of Architecture,
Venice Biennial 2002, photograph by Ramak Fazel

Translation
Globe, Foligno
Adam Victor for Scriptum, Rome

www.alessi.com

www.electaweb.it

Contents

Introduction

○ Since time immemorial the Alessi family has been firmly established on Lake Orta. We originally come from Luzzogno, the oldest village in the Strona valley. The first Alessi I've traced was called Giovanni; in 1633 he married a certain Caterina Gozano in Luzzogno. That's all I know about him, and I don't know a great deal more about the eight generations separating him from me. I nonetheless have no doubt that my forebears were among the

many men from the Strona valley who, in the seventeen hundreds, went as far as Germany to learn the trade of pewter-maker. Some of their number stayed on to make their fortune; others returned home and opened the first craft workshops. Such were the beginnings of the Omegna (and its suburb Crusinallo) makers of metal household objects, today one of the most dynamic centres in Europe for the production of such items.

△ Six members of the Alessi family, each with one of our most famous "mystery objects", Philippe Starck's *Juicy Salif* lemon squeezer. Sitting in the centre is Carlo; behind him, his brother Ettore, son Michele and nephew Stefano; sitting to his left is his son Alessio. I'm the one in the foreground.

ALESSI

△ The blue expanse
of Lake Orta from above.
Right, the outline of *Anna G.*,
the character created by
Alessandro Mendini as a
corkscrew, watching over
the Crusinallo plant.

△ In the Strona valley,
between the slopes of Monte
Rosa and the lake, traditions
retain a tenacious grip: a new
museum, the Omegna Forum,
gathers together the moving
testimonies of centuries of toil
and poetry.

The first metal household article manufacturer in the Cusio area was a man called Baldassarre Cane, who towards the mid-eighteen hundreds had the courage to leave Chesio (another small village in the Strona valley) for the lakeside and found the first true workshop. Although the company no longer exists, by around 1900 it was a large employer. In the following years his example was followed by many dozens of craftsmen/small businessmen, who often learned their trade as workmen at Cane's factory. Over the course of one and a half centuries, pewter has given way to other metals: brass, nickel silver, aluminium and then stainless steel, whose cycle of development is still running its course. Yet during this period neither the type nor the nature of the objects themselves have changed, and my town remains dominated by this industrial specialization. Along the shores of Lake San Giulio, amongst the Romanesque churches and the Baroque chapels, the household goods factories have become a precise point of reference, leaving their strong social and cultural imprint on the whole area. One of those early craftsmen/small businessmen was my grandfather, Giovanni Alessi. This book sets out to tell the tale of how a deep-rooted, hard, traditional and perhaps even inward-looking manufacturing tradition has blossomed into our own business venture, on the contrary characterized by constant innovation, open to experimentation and to the paradoxical results of casting from a poetic mould. How Alessi has changed from being a "Workshop for the working of brass and nickel silver plates, with foundry" (so read the sign over our stand at the first Milan Trade Fairs in the twenties) into one of the "factories of Italian design." The change from a metallurgical and mechanical industry into a workshop actively researching the field of applied arts has been

a gradual one over several decades. It has been an exciting process which, quite possibly, could serve as a possible model for the evolution of many kinds of industry in our consumer society. This too can be a reason to read on.

△ The *Omegna Tablet in Orthographic Characters*, designed by Luigi Serafini in 1985, is a wry, pseudo-archaeological look at the "meaning" of Alessi and its history.

The 1920s and 1930s

△ FAO, or Fratelli Alessi Omegna: the overlapping letters of the first historic logo with vaguely deco curves.

▽ Company founder Giovanni Alessi began as a particularly skilful maker of brass knobs.

○ Grandpa Giovanni was a talented sheet-metal worker. In 1921 he bought a plot of land at Omegna and founded Alessi. He started handmaking objects for the table and for the home in copper, brass and nickel silver, which were then either nickel-, chrome- or silver-plated. Grandpa was a real stickler for quality and for well-done work: the things he made quickly won acclaim for their workmanship and perfect finish.

△ Something of an epicure, Grandpa came away from long meals with inspiration for new objects. Here he is with his friend "Cichin" Lagostina.

▷ An engraving of the old factory at Crusinallo, set in the Alpine foothills. Today the scene looks like an industrial archaeological landscape.

▷ The first items produced by Alessi were inspired by the canons dictated by the most famous household goods companies at the start of the twentieth century, particularly Austrian and English factories. The materials (brass and nickel silver) are typical of household preferences during the twenties.

△ Alessi in the early days: the cleaning department. Items were manufactured to order, according to the specific requirements of the customer—a way of working still based on a crafts approach.

△ Engravings in the early catalogues are a time machine back to middle-class tastes of the day.

▷ An interesting example of a typical—now extinct—object on Italian tables between the two wars: a *Flask holder* (1925).

▽ Double services (teapot, coffee pot, sugar bowl and milk jug on a tray) are the mainstay of production.

ALESSI

▷ Starting in 1924 the Fratelli Alessi Omegna company began manufacturing coffee pots and trays, as well as small household items. Still no pots and pans or cutlery, items requiring more complex materials and processing.

△ The illustrations on these pages are based upon some of the objects found in the oldest Alessi catalogues, as reinterpreted by air-brush artist Tiger Tateishi in 1979.

▷ The quality of Giovanni Alessi's household articles improved rapidly, thanks to technical innovations such as chroming by galvanic bath, nickel-plating and silver-plating. These objects had the no-nonsense solidity of everyday common sense, finished with delicate and traditional ornamental elements.

◁ As Alessandro Mendini points out in his 1979 book *Paesaggio casalingo*, until the thirties developments within the company took the form of an analytical building up of standard objects. The catalogues (the earliest of which dates back to 1925) mark the start of an autonomous activity, showing a dense succession of crafted articles for coffee and tea, for the table, bars, and kitchens, corresponding to a highly polite and archaic way of eating. Objects of this kind are important more for sociological than aesthetic reasons; they have entered our collective past and our collective memory.

ALESSI

o Alessi

ALFRA

◁ The ALessi FRAtelli eagle brand logo took flight in 1947, replacing the old FAO acronym; it was to stay in use until 1967, when it gave way to the Ceselleria Alessi brand.

◁ The *Octagonal tea and coffee service* was a de rigueur presence in the possessions of a "proper family" (1935).

○ Design, as we understand the word today, first made its appearance with my father, Carlo. Trained as an industrial designer in Novara, he joined the company when still very young, dedicating himself to design right from the start. He was responsible for most of the objects made between the mid-thirties and 1945, the year he launched his last project, that archetype of early Italian design, called the *Bombé* tea and coffee sets. In the fifties he took over from Grandpa at the helm of the company, completely giving up (I have never understood why…) design.

◁ In the fifties my father (here strolling with Leo Oggioni, our first agent for Italy) transformed Alessi from a small business to a true industrial concern, dynamically expanding exports to encompass over sixty countries.

◁ Carlo photographed at the drawing board, during his military service.

During the war years, as the household goods market slowed down, Alessi produced stars for uniforms and mechanical parts for Savoia Marchetti aeroplanes. After the war, faced with an enormous demand for brass ladles for the U.S. army, my father doubled the number of machine tools, expanded the company and started mass-production. As he had realized so early, stainless steel was set to conquer the space vacated by chromed metals and silver-plated alloys.

△ *Oil cruet* and *Cheese cellar*, 1949 prototypes which were initial experiments into stainless steel. Below: a design I'm fond of for the simplicity of its forms, the *Cilindrico tea and coffee service* (1945), a contemporary of *Bombé*.

A L E S S I

The 1950s and 1960s

▽ Carrying on from the preceding decades under Ettore Alessi's technical guidance, the major push into the catering market: the handles and spouts in the *Dani* service (1963–98) are longer and more pronounced, as if to mirror the personality of objects which though practical are certainly not anonymous; the range includes coffee jugs and cream jugs.

○ Uncle Ettore, eleven years younger than his brother, joined my father in 1945. Although he no longer officially works for the company, he remains the great authority on cold pressing of metals. I affectionately refer to him as our "mega-technical director." As head of the technical department, in 1955 he opened Alessi up to collaboration with external designers; the work with architects Carlo Mazzeri, Luigi Massoni and Anselmo Vitale produced several ranges of objects, particularly for the catering trade, many of which are still big sellers.

△ The community service designed around the *101* coffee pot, in production since 1956, numbers twenty-eight different objects, and is the most professional and most popular line in the company's history.

▷ The introduction of stainless steel processing brought a number of structural and technical changes to the company.

△ The tray-forming department at the end of the forties. The machines are chiefly screw presses. Uncle Ettore, extremely young and almost impossible to recognise, is the last figure at the back, working on a lathe.

▷ Ettore Alessi strengthened the design identity of the company's technical office, paving the way for development of several best-selling products such as the range of wire *Baskets* and *Fruit bowls*. He oversaw a radical new shift in materials: brass and nickel silver made way for stainless steel, the new king of the household, first brought experimentally to Alessi by Carlo in the late thirties.

A L E S S I

▷ The wire *Citrus basket*, in
production from 1952, is a
veritable "industrial standard";
it symbolizes our fifties output.

△ Another winner in this period was the *Serving dish*, which has always been recurrent in the Alessi catalogue. The classic oval *110* dish was produced in eight sizes, from the smallest of 25 cm to the largest, which was 75 cm. Again for the hotel service is an extensive series of *Soup tureens*, *Legume dishes* and *Sauceboats*, produced in the early sixties, but directly derived from designs of the twenties.

△ A project approach means blending the artistic freedom of the designer with the concrete requirements of manufacturing. Inevitably, some ideas are destined not to progress beyond the design stage, such as this double *Sauceboat* designed by Joe Colombo and Ambrogio Pozzi.

A L E S S I

▽ Massoni and Mazzeri's objects are part of *Programme 4*, a cultural shift which introduced the concepts of "designer," "project" and indeed "design" to the world of household articles.

▷ In 1957, as part of the debate on the evolution of applied arts and nascent industrial design, the *Shaker*, *Ice bucket* and *Ice tongs* from *Programme 4* were selected and displayed at the 11th Milan Triennale Exhibition. For the first time, Alessi articles appeared in an exhibition on "designer" industrial production.

▷ The *Avio* (1961–98) series includes the tray pictured below. The name is not only a tip of the hat to airline companies, it is a homage to Alessi's history: mass manufacturing in the 1950s was only possible thanks to the supplies of aeronautics parts following the Second World War.

▽ In this "pre-'68" advertisement the Eiffel Tower is a rather ingenuous, but nevertheless explicit, signifier of internationality and class. Alessi steel articles gleam on a swish terrace, counterpoised perhaps involuntarily, but most certainly effectively, against the most spectacular modern symbol of metal use.

A L E S S I

The 1970s

○ Officially my career at Alessi began in July 1970, the day after I graduated in law. My dad immediately set me to work on new projects. I threw myself into the job. With a strongly utopian view of "multiplied art," I developed my cultural-theoretic manifesto championing a new commercial civilization offering the consuming masses veritable artistic items at low prices.

△ The designers signed up for the "art multiples" were Italian sculptors Giò Pomodoro, Carmelo Cappello, Pietro Consagra and Andrea Cascella, with Yugoslav Dušan Džamonja. The process was a kind of collective madness which tied up our mechanical workshop for almost three years. Staring at the Salvador Dalí prototype my father decided the moment had come to pull the plug on the escapade: but I had already bought the 50,000 steel hooks to manufacture the first 1000 multiples...

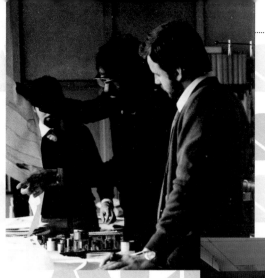

◁ Franco Sargiani and Eija Helander are the first designers I brought to Alessi. The partnership with them extended to graphic design, packaging and stand design, as well as part of the Crusinallo offices. Attempting to rationalize fundamental aspects of corporate life was a huge job. The new *Alessi* logotype began to be used in 1971.

△ Here the Alessi stands designed by the Sargiani-Helander duo in the early seventies.

△ The company offices at Crusinallo are also a Franco Sargiani collaboration.

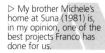

▷ My brother Michele's home at Suna (1981) is, in my opinion, one of the best projects Franco has done for us.

▽ A strong bond grew with the extrovert and enthusiastic Franco. Development of *Programme 8* took five years. The basic idea: total component mobility of basically square or rectangular objects, which were difficult to manufacture in steel. A true international innovation in household objects in the seventies, it was backed up by a major advertising campaign.

◁ In 1972 Sargiani accepted the request to introduce me to some top designers to launch *Programme 7*. The first contacts were with the Milan-based Exhibition design group. Under the leadership of Silvio Coppola (left), Pino Tovaglia, Franco Grignani, Giulio Confalonieri and Bruno Munari all worked for us, though the resulting designs didn't ever see the light of day. With hindsight, I recognize that those objects still belonged to the "Bel design Italiano" style of the sixties.

SILVIO COPPOLA

△ The *Tiffany* tray (1974–97) symbolized the range: 10,000 items per year, and a turnover which cheered the intolerant and ferocious Coppola. Sales this big were of huge importance to me: I had proved that designer items could sell well! It was around that time that Dad started going fishing every Thursday.

◁ Coppola's baskets and trays combine tightly packed graphic analysis complete with minuscule handwritten notes, and an innovative use of technological research. His work focused on finding new ways to perforate and shape steel sheeting, wire and gratings. This series had a tough genesis, particularly because of how complex it was to mount the objects, but the public response was extremely encouraging: Tovaglia's *Teorema* tray (1973–1994), Confalonieri's *Maya* basket (1977) and Coppola's *Square* basket (1977–1995) provided us with a balanced and, in its own way, classic form of high quality "modern" style, which was by no means too extravagant.

ALESSI

Ettore Sottsass

" *I think it is very hard to design a 'beautiful table': it does not depend simply on the tools and materials one uses, it also depends on a subtle, fragile and uncertain sagacity which, sometimes, somebody—who knows how and who knows why—manages to channel into the design: the total perception of our cosmic adventure, as fleeting, ineffable and incomprehensible as it may be.* "

○ Ettore Sottsass came to Crusinallo in 1972, on Sargiani's invitation. Uncle Ettore and I met him; I was really impressed. He was preceded by the fame of his work for Olivetti, his reputation as the guru of radical design, and he was the first person of truly international standing with whom I had dealings. He is something of a philosopher, bursting with charisma, and he has something interesting to say about everything. It was with him that I began talking over the "high" topics of design, the role of industry in society. Although we meet up only once in a while —due to a certain shyness on my part, as if I was afraid of using up the relationship with him—he was the first person I met through work who for me has become a real mentor, one of my maestros.

▷ One truly unique range: the professional articles for the bar and for serving wine, designed by Sottsass in 1979 with assistance from Alberto Gozzi, taking a cue from the perfect cocktails prepared with such expertise by David Niven in those fifties movies.

▽ The range takes its name from the American shaker (*Boston*), and includes the *Wine cooler* in two versions (for Bordeaux style or for magnums), supplied— if requested—with a special *Stand*, *Strainer*, *Ice tongs* and *Stirrer*.

A L E S S I

▷ A homage to Gauguin intimated in this ad conveys the impression that Sottsass's *Holder and oven-to-table porcelain dish* is an instant classic: technical and stylistic details in common with the *5070* condiment set.

▽ Sottsass does not discriminate between materials: he is one of the most prolific designers in wood, as in his late eighties Twergi line.

▽ The *Tray*, or to be precise the rectangular "fancy tray" (1982) is a subtle Sottsass challenge for Alessi; he well knows how difficult it is to manufacture stainless steel in boxy shapes.

Design Ettore Sottsass, 1994

...eto portapirofila · Holder and oven-to-table dish · Support et plat ...orzellanschale mit Gestell · Conjunto porta-fuente con fuente

◁ The first items Sottsass designed for Alessi were large, wide-rimmed trays: we quickly decided that was not the right direction, and we asked him to tackle oil cruets. With his Finnish assistant Ulla Salovaara he soon came up with the *5070* condiment set (1978), one of our best designs of the last twenty years, and certainly one of our articles that comes closest to being an "industrial standard." Despite being relatively expensive, this little table-top mosque is our best-selling steel condiment set.

▽ The *Butter dish* is in stainless steel and crystal: it was a 1998 addition to the *Oil cruet and cruet service* dated 1978.

△ *La Bella Tavola* porcelain service saw the light of day in 1993. Sottsass designed this in pure white lines, or in a version with subtle, classic, overlapping blue lines.

◁ Alighiero Boetti, one of Italy's most original contemporary artists, had his curiosity piqued by the idea, and by the broad spaces left on the ornamental edges. He came up with an elaborate decoration, unique in its use of so many shapes and colours.

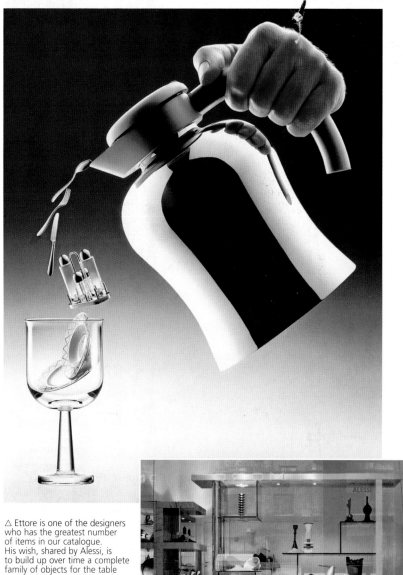

△ Ettore is one of the designers who has the greatest number of items in our catalogue. His wish, shared by Alessi, is to build up over time a complete family of objects for the table and the kitchen, as did Josef Hoffmann for Wiener Werkstätte.

▷ Sottsass is also the man responsible for the first Alessi *Flagship* in Milan (1987), refurbished in 1999 by the Atelier Mendini (see "The Wonder Shops" chapter).

A L E S S I

◁ The *Ginevra* range of glasses is dedicated to the pleasures of "fine drinking." The new version of these crystal glasses (2003) will constitute the missing link in Sottsass's design project for Alessi tableware. As well as glasses and goblets of varying sizes, there is also a *Decanter*, so beloved of the connoisseur.

△ Sottsass's ambition is becoming a reality: to design an entire table place setting, *a very gracious way of demonstrating awareness, respect and care for the* basic *event of nutrition*.

▽ Designed in 1987, with the assistance of Alberto Gozzi, the *Nuovo Milano* cutlery set has become a classic, winning the XVIth Compasso d'oro award.

Richard Sapper

○ Richard first came to Crusinallo on Shrove Tuesday, 1977. Ettore Sottsass recommended him in these terms: *He's the Tizio lamp guy, the guy who has never done a bad design.* Dad, Uncle Ettore and I greeted him. He was dressed all in black and wearing a bizarre piper's hat. Sapper usually works on just a few designs at a time, only things that really interest him; it's hard to force him into a narrow brief: far better to give him free reign, at a rate of roughly one new project every five years.

△ Sapper has designed some items which have become historic not just in design terms, but also for Alessi's economic fortunes: the *9090* coffee pot (see p. 32). Launched in 1979, this was Alessi's first project for the kitchen; until then we had focused only on objects for the dining and living room.

◁ RS07 (2002), an electric version of the three-cup 9090 coffee pot. A handy travel set is also available for those travellers who can't manage without their real espresso coffee when away from home.

▷ Two flagship Sapper designs for Alessi: coffee pot *9090* (the first coffee pot manufactured at Crusinallo, awarded the XIth Compasso d'oro and on display at the MoMA in New York), and the majestic *Kettle with a singing whistle*, inspired by the sound of the steamers and barges that ply the Rhine, the first "designer" kettle (1982).

▷ The *Kettle* is characterized by two pitch-pipes in "E" and "B" lodged in the brass whistle pipes. Small devices commonly used to tune musical instruments, they are specially made for us by craftsmen in the Black Forest.

▷ A real thorn in the side of our engineers, Sapper's presence in the company has to be carefully regulated to prevent sparks flying. In the best Ulm school tradition— "the designer must, by definition, know the technology he works with intimately"—Sapper considers himself an expert on every manufacturing topic: because of the countless hard-to-make details in his designs, he gets into long and hotly contested arguments with the engineers. The results are stunning: the *Bandung* "automatic" tea maker, (right, produced from 1995 to 2000) and his most recent project, the *Cobán* electric coffee maker, which aroused the same feelings in me when I saw its earliest prototype as the *9090* coffee pot did, eighteen years ago.

◁ The *Cobán* (1997) was launched in four versions to cater to the personal tastes of vast numbers of coffee drinkers. The two traditional versions (with and without coffee grinder) are joined by two innovative ones using prepacked, easy-to-use coffee doses: the *Nespresso*, which uses proprietary coffee portion doses, and the *Easy Serving Espresso*, which takes E.S.E. single use coffee portions (both 1998).

A L E S S I

Sapper is also the man behind the most complex project I have ever worked on: *The Cintura di Orione* range of cooking utensils, made possible thanks to Alberto Gozzi's fundamental help and designed to accommodate the suggestions of several famous French and Italian chefs and experts in European cookery. The research was launched in 1979 and dedicated to the "private gourmet" public, namely those enthusiasts of intelligent and creative cooking who are often led to use some borderline professional utensils because of their culinary passion. That is why most recipients are produced in special dual lamina (outside extra thick copper + inside in 18/10 stainless steel), which offers a more professional performance and allows to recover in modern cooking the advantages of copper as far as conduction and homogeneous distribution of heat are concerned. These features are paired with extremely hygienic stainless steel inside.

▷ **Roger Vergé**

Blending innovation and tradition, he finished off the unusual large oval-shaped *Fish poacher with rack* (60 centimetres long), ideal for cooking fish of varying sizes, as well as pig's trotters.

◁ **Thuilier & Charial**

The godfather of French cuisine was a consultant on the *Oval casserole*, a cast iron pot ideal for slow cooking stews and braised meats. The strong material and heavy lid keep in all the steam and flavours.

▷ Pierre and Michel Troisgros

The Lyon-based masters in Nouvelle
Cuisine worked on the *Black-iron
frying pans* (curves specially designed
to facilitate omelet flip acrobatics),
the *Long-handled saucepan*,
and the delightful single-serving
Cassolette.

▽ Gualtiero Marchesi

The Italian "creative chef"
par excellence worked on the
more traditional items, such
as the *Stockpot* and the two
copper and steel *Casseroles*.

A L E S S I

2003 brings important news for the *Cintura di Orione*. On one hand two new items are being presented: the *Shallow Long-handled Pan* or *Sautoir* and the *Oval Pan with Lid*, perfected with the expertise of Alberto Gozzi.

On the other hand, a new triple-lamina version has been introduced for several articles (outside in AISI 304 steel + extra-thick aluminum + inside in 18/10 stainless steel). This version comes very close to the unbeatable heat conduction of the copper version, compared to which it has the advantages of being easier to clean, useable on electromagnetic induction heat sources, and of being much more economical to buy.

△ **Angelo Paracucchi**

A great exponent of Mediterranean cooking, he worked with Sapper on the *Flambé pan* and *Lamp*, objects right out of the spectacular tradition of the Belle Époque, re-invented in a modern interpretation.

◁ **Alain Chapel**

The undisputed international authority on sauces worked on the copper and steel *Sauteuse* with flared sides, adding a *Whisk* for beating and mixing.

◁ **Alberto Gozzi**

Alberto Gozzi, the top gourmet, has assisted Alessi on a number of projects with his gastronomic expertise. He was also the enthusiastic coordinator for the research that spawned this series of utensils. A few years back the President of the Italian Re-

public "stole" him from us and took him off to Rome, where he manages the Quirinal Palace's catering service. Nevertheless, he continues to pass his priceless advice on to us, as can be seen from the new recipients presented in 2003: *Shallow, Long-handled Pan* or *Sautoir* and the *Oval Pan with Lid*.

Achille Castiglioni

❝ *Naturally, Alessi design concept is so broad that there was just the right space and positioning for my own design concept. And I feel great in this space… this element of enjoyment is an integral part of both my own and Alessi's design.* ❞

○ I clearly remember the first time I met this great legend of Italian design, Castiglioni, in his Milan studio at Piazza Castello: we soon worked out a possible area of collaboration, the *Dry* service range of cutlery. I consider Castiglioni a great master, a man of insatiable curiosity, blessed with great irony and exceptional modesty; a man who can design masterpieces. He is very realistic, like the good Milanese gent he is, and he understands his audience well. The best way to get him to work is to bring him an idea that tickles him. Our best ideas have come to us late in the evening, over a tumbler of whisky. Achille died in December 2002. Vittorio Gregotti wrote that we always expect him to appear at any minute, soon… But actually he is always with us, for his extraordinary lesson of intelligence, humility and levity, lingers on in each one of us.

▷ The three Castiglioni brothers in sporting garb, in a drawing/caricature from the thirties.

▽ The *Fruit bowl-colander* (1995) responds to two fundamentals for Castiglioni: providing a practical solution to small "dining at table" problems, where possible with a small but intelligent functional innovation, plus the people's preference for a polished metal finish. In a broad Milanese accent, Castiglioni sums up: *cinc ghèi pussée, ma luster (five lire more, but shiny).*

◁ To solve the *Ashtray* conundrum—torment and delight of many a designer—Castiglioni, an absent-minded smoker, provides an ingenious solution: a spiral spring (easy to extract for cleaning) holds the cigarette and prevents it from falling (1970).

▽ *Foldable tray*, with retractable sections to vary its dimensions, never went into production (1982).

▽ Over thirty years separate the two designs in this photo, both manufactured in 1996: the *Ondula* fruit bowl and *Firenze* wall clock, designed with his brother Pier Giacomo for the 1965 "La casa abitata" exhibition held at Palazzo Strozzi, Florence.

A L E S S I

◁ These glasses are another classic project begun with his brother Pier Giacomo: the original design dates back to 1965, but Achille updated it and come up with some new items, after collaborating with well-known wine and food expert Luigi Veronelli, who also created the name *Orseggi* (1997, 1999, 2001).

▽ The *Splügen* beer glass and bottle opener are a 2001 reproduction of two classic Castiglione designs, originally produced in 1960 for the Splügen Brau bar project in Milan.

◁ The *Grand Prix* cutlery set won the first prize in the competition held by Gio Ponti for Reed & Barton in 1960, but was never produced, probably because of the extreme technical complexity of making the knife. The set has been included in the catalogue since 1997.

▽ The *Dry* service marked our debut in cutlery manufacture (1982).

A L E S S I

△ The *Bavero* (1997) porcelain service, displayed here on the workbench, is another superb specimen of Castiglioni's work. This project draws its raison d'être from what the architect refers to as "the principal design element," in other words the key project idea that the designer must seize the intuition at the start of any job: in this case, it's a simple (but highly significant, not to say bold) design move—folding the edges of the plates downwards.

▽ For the 2001 *Bavero* service is born *Tea for Two*, based upon the nice and extremely practical *Cabaré* melamine tray.

△ Such has been the success of *Bavero* that in 2001 we started launching new items for the service, plus a decorated version. Once again, the *à la Castiglioni* treatment is expressed through the simple decision to apply light azure to the folds of certain items in the service.

◁ Castiglioni's sense of practicality, his attention to everyday whims, come out in the *Mayonnaise spoon*, conceived specially for scooping up the stuff that sticks to the inside of the jar. This spoon was originally designed with Pier Giacomo in 1962 as a promotional gadget for Kraft, and manufactured by us in 1997.

▽ Picking up on the theme of ready-made, this prototype seven-armed candelabra is called *Menorah*, and rests on the rubber covering of a Japanese motorbike grip. Three of them were produced in 1985 for the "Nerot Mitzvah, Contemporary Ideas for Light in the Jewish Ritual" research project, promoted by our common friend Izzika Gaon of the Israel Museum in Jerusalem.

△ These *Cruets* for oil and vinegar with counter-weighted lid, designed in 1980, have become a quintessential classic of the Castiglioni style.

A L E S S I

Alessandro Mendini

> " *If it is to be organic and justifiable, the design of a flow of products must be conducted from within a 'critical awareness' of one's own story; this is the pre-condition for diagnosis and planning ahead.* "

BOOK

PAESAGGIO CASALINGO

STARCK OFFICINA

○ It is by no means easy to describe Alessandro Mendini's relations with myself and Alessi. What I can say is that for me he has been the master, in a vaguely Socratic fashion, who has gradually introduced me to the many mysteries of our fascinating profession. When people ask me what Mendini does for us, what his role is, I can only smile: Sandro is such a *sui generis* consultant that his position cannot really be described outside its context: a relationship similar to Peter Behrens' with AEG of Rathenau.

SAX

Mendini began working with us in 1977 when, under his guidance, a design and architecture magazine destined to make quite a stir over the following years, *Modo*, first started.

△ It is Mendini who designed my living space, the "House of Happiness." As well as drawing the plan (above), Alessandro coordinated the work of the other architects involved.

△ The limited series *Vaso Viso*, a great ceramic vase, one of the strong points of Alessandro's personal exhibition at the Fondation Cartier, in Paris, Spring 2002.

△ *Candlestick Flame* (2002). The spiralling Totem/Colonna is a recurring theme in many of Sandro's projects from the 1970s onwards. In my personal interpretation of his work, the Colonna opens the gates of Eden, that earthly paradise we are all seeking, paradise made of harmony and good, beautiful things, whilst the serpentine evolution of Tortiglione is symbolic of temptation, ambiguity in the world...

▷ *Cioccolator*: this calculator does not set out to make maths better, its purpose is simply to put the fun back into numerical calculations, to banish the lack of emotional connection in an activity all too often performed with aesthetically and sensorially deficient tools (2000).

▷ Somehow, in an extremely informal way, Mendini is aware of our most intimate problems and wishes. Actually, without even meeting up that often, over the years we have perfected a way of working together that is almost telepathic…

SERVIZIO PIATTI

A·ALESSI
A·MENDINI

VENTI ANNI DI COLLABORAZIONE

◁ In 1996 began the production of the porcelain dinner services designed by Mendini with Annalisa Margarini. Alessandro presented the basic service in white, *How much white*, the *How many stars* version, with delicate gilt decoration, and the pointillist decoration *Proust* (2001), whilst the polychrome triangles of the lively *How many colours* decoration are by Nicola De Maria.

ALESSANDRO MENDINI

○ Author of the research project *Paesaggio casalingo* and other books, Mendini is Alessi's official chronicler. As a designer, he continues to design objects, often in the most complex and exciting areas of our catalogue. As an architect, he has designed my home (the "house of happiness"), two extensions for the factory at Crusinallo, the Alessi Museum and the layout of several exhibitions. In his role as design manager he has been responsible for the invention and coordination of some of our most legendary design processes, a few of which are illustrated here. As a consultant, he has brought to my attention a huge number of designers who have gone on to work with us.

△ The popular *Recinto* family (born in 1997) of trays and baskets with a scalloped border. It's plain to see that the trays are tremble-proof, thanks to thick handles for a better grip, and a "safety" edge: in profile, they hint at generous giving, the transfer from inside to outside, though not without a hint of self-mockery.

△ *Anna Set* (2001): this Mendinian interpretation of the central European and Anglo-Saxon creamer and sugar set is a point of cross-over between Alessi's two most famous families: *Anna* and *Recinto*.

▷ A limited edition collection of mosaic *Recinto* trays: a joint project for 2000, with mosaic specialist Bisazza from the Veneto region.

ALESSI

▽ The *Anna Cheese* (1999) grater is an interesting departure from all the other graters we make: the grater itself revolves around the piece of cheese. Mendini drew his inspiration from a classic grater made in Savoy, with teeth cut the Italian way, ideal for grating parmesan and other hard cheeses.

△ *Anna Stop* stopper (1999).

◁ *Anna Pepper* peppermill (1998).

▽ *Anna Light* lighter (1998).

△ *Anna Box* box (1999).

Alessi. Extra ordinary.

▷ The extraordinary success of the corkscrew made it inevitable that the popular *Anna* icon would grow into a small family. Her cult status is wittily underlined in this Lowe Lintas Pirella Göttsche advert, which has her depicted as a new Marilyn for the twenty-first century.

▷ I'm especially proud of the *Anna G.* corkscrew (1994), which immediately became our top bestseller, thereby debunking the rumour (slyly put about by the man himself) that Mendini only designs objects that don't sell!

◁ *Anna Time* timer (1999).

△ Alessi's Crusinallo
headquarters bears the mark
of the Atelier Mendini,
with a vital contribution by
Francesco Mendini: here,
the plan for extension,
and the reception area stairs
leading to the exhibition hall
(1995).

◁ The allusive
Alessi stand
at the Frankfurt Fair.

ALESSI

△ The Omegna Forum, the new museum of local arts and traditions (1998), designed by the Atelier Mendini.

◁ The conference room at Alessi's Hamburg offices, a Mendini design too, with the reassuring shapes of the *100% Make Up* vases (1996).

▷ Mendini's most recent project: the Alessi installation at Studio Più in Milan during Macef, in September 2001.

Tea & Coffee Piazza

△ Robert Venturi's objects, marked by their subtle decoration, are set on a tray reproducing Piazza del Campidoglio.

○ In 1979 Alessandro Mendini's exuberant mind came up with the idea of setting "pure" architects the task of designing an object, the classic tea and coffee service. Produced in a run of ninety-nine each, the eleven silver services came out with the Officina Alessi brand and the designer's monogram. In 1983 they were presented to the public in an exhibition arranged by Hans Hollein at the San Carpoforo church in Milan.

△ Japanese logic and precision for Kazumasa Yamashita: the knobs of these recipients form the initials of their contents.

◁ Ironic and eclectic postmodern style for Charles Jencks, who designs extravagant tubby columns with capitals, somewhere between surprise and parody.

ALESSI

With this project Aldo Rossi demonstrates his talents as a designer: the tray turns into a home tabernacle to officiate the hospitable rite of coffee.

▽ Paolo Portoghesi uses hexagons and pyramids to sculpt a domestic citadel for those little pleasures, even—the only designer to do so—adding an ash tray for smokers.

▽ It's all curves in Alessandro Mendini's design, which seems to breathe new life into the timeless *Bombé*: the articles are ready to leap from their slender pedestals.

▽ Viewed from above, Michael Graves's objects recall the outline of biscuits, expressing their convivial appearance in the refined materials.

▽ Oscar Tusquets's objects consist of two soldered shells with riveting in relief along an oblique axis.

▽ Hans Hollein fits his items along one side of a tray recalling the bridge of an aircraft carrier; Hollein also designed the "wall" for displaying the eleven services.

▽ Eerie little hands poke out of Stanley Tigerman's tray, while the spouts are shaped as inviting half-open lips (a detail requiring a high-risk technical approach).

The *Tea & Coffee Piazza* series takes up and develops two major themes: the concept of "artistic multiple" and the involvement of international architects in the quest for design. This feature was strongly promoted by Mendini, who foretold the end of "bel design italiano" and, setting himself "at the crossroads between the awareness of tradition and the lure of the unknown," felt the need to go back to the roots of the phenomenon of design, to the fifties, when "pure" architects began to design objects. Indeed, not only did this venture start off the trend of highly expressive, postmodern, style-symbol "objects of emotion"; it enabled me to make an incredible number of contacts and have new experiences which would come in very handy for the product policy of the following years. As a research venture, we owe it the discovery of two great new designers: Aldo Rossi and Michael Graves.

▽ Richard Meier studied a complex integration of square volumes and rounded forms, in a brilliant play of inside and outside, container and contents.

Aldo Rossi

○ Aldo Rossi was a lake-lover like me. He was never happier than when he went to meditate and write at the old family house on Lake Mergozzo, I found out when we first met in the spring of 1980. He designed some of the most representative of our eighties articles, and had an ability—which only the great designers have—to tune in to the public mood. Rossi regarded design as something of a hobby; his first love was always architecture. He died in an accident on Lake Maggiore. The first of my masters to pass away. I miss him terribly, I'm very sad to say.

" *I feel there is often something mysterious in the process of selling objects: sometimes I see objects as clay relics ranged in museums; a material enclosing a world that perhaps merely desires to be used and destroyed. There are always two ways of looking at things.*

▷ The *Momento* range of watches (1987) is the only one still in the Alessi catalogue. Aldo loved watches and clocks, often incorporating them into his public buildings.

◁ Rossi's dream was to produce a new Moka to sell all, if possible at a low price: he got very close with his *La cupola* aluminium espresso coffee maker (1988).

◁ Throughout August 1997 I kept the prototype of his *Pitcher* in my car: I knew that Aldo was due to come to Lake Maggiore, and he would have been happy to see it. He never got the chance.

▽ The *Press filter coffee maker* made during the research that resulted in *Cupola* (1986).

As can be seen from the design of a coffee-maker "protected" by *San Carlone* of Arona, Aldo had a way of relating to our engineers that was worlds away from what we had experienced: he made sketches, presented them, and then waited for the engineers to make all their comments and changes, even sweeping ones.
It seemed as if everything was OK! For my Uncle and Casalino, fresh from the relationship with Sapper, this was a scandalous attitude. One day Uncle even said to him in his grumpy way: *But, really, couldn't you bring us finished designs rather than these sketches which are only half done?*
That was the only time I ever saw Rossi get angry. He answered dryly that if we wanted final-draft technical designs, then we could get them from Zanuso, but not from him. Rossi's attitude helped me to understand an approach to design not restricted to himself, but shared to some degree by all or almost all designers who have experience as architects.

il ritorno dalla scu[...]

△ The book *La conica e altre caffettiere* (1984) is the result of his research into the making and serving of coffee.

◁ Rossi's designs always reveal an (often playful, always explanatory) relationship between the design object and constructive architecture.

▷ *La Conica*, which Rossi designed between 1980 and 1983, started life as an evolution of Aldo's contribution to the *Tea & Coffee Piazza* project, translating a precious silver object into a mass-produceable steel product, with the new attributes of solidity and ease of use. Initially Rossi was a little wary of industry in general, but he liked Alessi and he threw himself into long research projects regarding coffee-related items, which were to become a kind of obsession for him: notes, sketches, photographs, designs, multifarious projects such as the percolator, the *New Orleans* model and that for American-style coffee... For Rossi the coffee maker (finally produced in two versions, *conical* and *domed*, from 1984) perfectly symbolized the dialectic relation between architecture (better still, town planning) and the "household landscape" into which this miniature monument fits.

▽ Beyond coffee makers, Rossi's work for Alessi is eclectic to say the least, spanning from wristwatches and wall clocks to the tower-belvedere designed for the "House of Happiness", yet to be built and here shown in photo-montage.

△ *La cubica*, in cast aluminium, is Aldo's homage to the saying *Form follows function*: it is the ideal utensil for cooking cubic tomatoes. Because of the great technical challenges and the high production costs, only a few hundred were produced, from 1991 to 2000.

▷ Rossi started out from a formal and expressive "strong idea," capable of resisting all the modifications required by the engineers: *You know far better than I how to make a coffee maker*, Aldo said to a speechless Casalino. This attitude of delegating the manufacturing details is why it is much easier and more relaxing for our engineers to work with architects rather than designers.

▽ The large steel pan
La Cupola, with double copper
bottom: designed in 1997,
in production from 2001.

In the days of the "famous" clash over technical drawings, my uncle was bewildered, but at the next opportunity he managed to redeem himself by comparing Aldo's designs to those of Morandi. Aldo was struck, and from that moment a great passion grew between the two of them, culminating in the design for my cousin Stefano's house at Suna (1995).

ALESSI

Michael Graves

" With Alessi, tradition extends to the idea of family. As a designer you and your people are brought in and treated as member of a family—it's a very personal relationship of designer and manufacturer. This is what ties everything. "

○ As early as January 1980, during our first visit to his big studio in Princeton, Michael Graves told us that from then on he would be spending at least half his time on design. It was a definitive statement which, moreover, corresponded to his great potential in this field. Michael does not like theory, even though he once confessed his desire to develop an "American" design. In any case, between the eighties and the nineties he showed an incredible ability to tune in to the tastes of even the average public: for this reason I consider him to be a forerunner of "Super & Popular."

▷ The 1985 *Kettle with bird* continues to go from strength to strength. It spawned a "family" of objects which Graves dauntlessly continues to expand, year after year, developing his own sensitivity towards a less intellectualized approach to design, softer than its European equivalents.

Graves' highly personal and easy to recognize formal style blends influences from the European tradition, Art Deco, American "pop," and flashes of pre-Columbian culture. He has shown he can bewitch the public like only very few of the designers with whom I've worked. I think that his success derives from his wholly uninhibited approach to the economic dimension which this activity inevitably entails.

△ The *Bollitore elettrico* (2001) is the popular electric version of the 1985 best-seller, clamoured for by our most typical tea drinker markets.

▷ *Press filter coffee maker, Demitasse cup, Mug, Butter dish:* an unmistakable look for objects well shielded by rings of steel, with easy-grip handles, ideal for those drowsy, half-asleep breakfasts (1989).

◁ *Pelicano* (1995): Graves also tackled the theme of the cast aluminium coffee percolator.

◁ *Pepper mill* (1988), *Salt castor* (1990) and *Kitchen timer* (1992): for Graves the concept of "family" spans a horizon of different items, every year increasing in extent, right down to the tiniest of pieces.

◁ The slim *Pepper mill* (1993) is one of the *Twergi* objects.

▽ This *Kitchen oil cruet* (2000) is a recent example of Graves in his finest pop mode.

▷ The *Cheese board* (1997) rests on a broad steel tray, and is made up of a ceramic cutting board "with holes," crowned by a transparent cover: the handle is a smiling mouse.

A L E S S I

▷ The *Bread bin* (1997) takes us back to a special spot in Graves's memory: the paunchy recipient is replete with nostalgia for the breakfast American children used to eat before the ready-made snack age, when it was an indispensable treasure chest guarding the aroma of freshly baked bread.

◁ The articles in the "Graves Family" came to life concentrically, developing around the *Kettle*, which was initially joined by the *Cream Jug* and the *Sugar Bowl* (1988). The large *Carafe* is dated 1991, the *Corkscrew* and the *Champagne Stopper* are from 1995.

◁ The *Oval Tray* with polyamide handles (1994) is one of the largest trays ever produced by Alessi.

Other Designers

○ I have worked with hundreds of designers since the early seventies. This has been the most rewarding experience of my life, and I continue to be thrilled by it. I am a lucky man: each of these encounters has left me with something of importance. I love seeing how, each time, the Vastness of the Creative Possible gels into images, words, gestures and thoughts, always unique, yet always focused on the heroic exploit of expressing something that is larger than we are. I am yet to understand the mysterious way that some of these designers have built up families in our catalogue, while many others have seemingly left a more fleeting trace... But what I do know is that just one project is all it takes to add something to this great game of life.

△ *Babyboop Vase* (2002): a handsome vase-sculpture and a remarkable challenge for our technicians, a pure Arad-style statement.

◁ *Babyboop* (2000) is the first design Ron has made for us in steel. It's a set of three small containers for nibbles, shaped to reflect the large blow-molded aluminium furniture/sculptures he made in a limited run in the late nineties.

Riccardo Dalisi

▷ His research into the
Neapolitan coffee maker
(1979–87, winning the
XIIth Compasso d'Oro) was
the longest in our history:
over the years it led to one
book and over two hundred
fully working prototypes in tin.
Wearing a beret and clothes
straight out of a neorealist
film, continuously turning over
new ideas and trying out new
ways of making things work,
Dalisi has not been an easy
person to manage, but this
was a very important project
for us indeed. It enabled us
to open up our manufacturing
world even more to the
conceptual experience of the
artisan; it taught us to dilute
our certainties in a fragile
and poetic light, which
is so necessary to work
on extremely deep-rooted
household rituals.

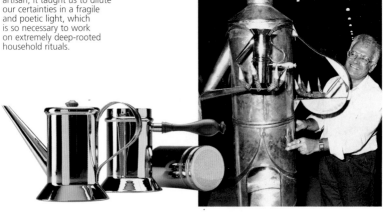

Andrea Branzi

« Building a house for somebody means building a place and objects with which one can enter in relations, not just of use and functionality, but also psychological, symbolic and poetic. Holderlin used to say Man lives poetically, which means that the relations that link a person to his nest are literary in nature—partly obscure— and symbolic. »

▽ A designer who requires the public at large to meet him halfway, as Branzi himself will not deny; but what can you say when a simple *Solferino* (2000) openwork citrus holder such as this encapsulates the finest features that twentieth-century contemporary art has to offer?

◁ *Mama-ò*, Branzi's kettle designed in 1988, has two symmetrical spouts with a melodic whistle, connected by a long handle.

▽ Concerned about ecology and natural forms, Branzi is one of the designers most sensitive to the turned wood of *Twergi*. His family, recognizable by their lengthened, linked lozenge decoration also includes the witty *Toothpick holder* (1991) and the *Bottle-opener* (1999).

ALESSI

△ Andrea has many interests, including this one of being an amateur horticulturist of rare flowering plant species: hence the inspiration of the charming series of vases *Terracina*, *Gibilterra* and *Volterra* (2002).

▽ Inevitably drawn from Branzi's own life (he has three sisters who married three brothers), is his passion for family trees and for "judicious couplings." Branzi has patiently and diligently collated and illustrated his *Genetic Tales* into a book. With complete lack of modesty he defines it a catalogue *collecting (almost) all examples of men*

alive at this end of the millennium. This research has resulted in a family of objects ranging from the *T-shirt* to the *Mug*. This tall (100 cm) vase is in many ways the patriarch of the *Genetic Tales* line. It was produced in a limited edition of ninety-nine in 1999. On a reduced scale, the *Small Vase* (2000), 20 cm high, was created. Each vase in this limited edition of 99,999 is unique.

Mario Botta

▷ "No preciousness, no
pedantic pernicketiness, no
evident sophistry: Botta's style
is modest, balanced, and never
convoluted." (F. Chaslin, 1982)
Mia and *Tua* (2000) are two
large carafes for water and
wine—the first Alessi
household project by this
Swiss architect since his
Eye watch (1989–97).

◁ *Tronco* (2002) flower
vase: heartfelt thanks
to Mario for this design
and also to Raimondo
Bianchi, the Milan florist
who made available his
experience and sensitivity
for hands-on trials
and for exploring the
expressive combinations
generated by vases and
the world of flowers.

Paolo Portoghesi

▷ The interwoven chapel arches of
Achphat in Armenia and the subtle
lines of the Tlemcen mosque
in North Africa have inspired
this micro-architecture, where
Portoghesi's trademark bundle
of lines culminates in the magical
light of a candle (1988–98).

Foster

...gular ...minium tray (1998), Foster returns to the essential, streamlined simplicity of certain Japanese objects, such as the low-slung futon. This simplicity in everyday gestures (handing things out, or sleeping) is reflected in the extremely subtle curve, which lends a relaxing gentleness to the tray silhouette.
Rack (2000) is the indispensable accessory for wall-hanging this outsize tray.

Frank Gehry

▽ *Pito* is the kettle designed by Gehry, with a mahogany handle and melodic stopper.

" *When the artists and sculptors I know are working, there is always an element of play involved. They experiment, try things out. A slightly naïve and infantile way of doing things, like children playing in a sandbox. Scientists work in a similar way. It's like casting away baggage until one is free to follow ideas, rather ...ing to see where one ... '* **"**

Jasper Morrison

○ What I like about Morrison is the courage and modesty he brings to his life as a designer. He knows only too well that in our field major innovation hardly ever comes about from great leaps forward, but rather it is the result of small and progressive improvements, dominated by the rich and fertile terrain of ancient rituals.

△ *Socrates* is a corkscrew (1998): the philosopher's maieutics strike again, providing expression of the ideas within the person/object with whom you have a dialogue.

▽ Interactivity, solutions for two objects which can be brought together: *Op* is a tray; *Op-la* turns into a table-tray with a stainless steel base (1998).

△ The *Twin salad bowl* (1998) is all the more striking for the simple archetypal elegance of its form, produced by the functional invention of a twin cover, and for the precision with which one approaches the gesture of serving-offering. The small notch in the edge of the bowl is designed for a thumb, to give extra grip, or as a recess for *Salad servers*.

▷ Casbah, sweet casbah... *Pepe le Moko* (1998) grinds sea salt and various types of peppercorns.

ALESSI

△ In this complete series
of *Ladles* and other accessories
to hang on the *Rack* (2002),
Jasper really has found the most
essential "ladleness"! The ladles
we dream of are right here,
and we cannot manage
without them.

◁ For many years I was
on the lookout for a good
contemporary design for a new
serving dish that not only met all
professional catering standards,
but had a design that made it
suited to home use too.
I personally find that there is no
better serving dish than a nice
big stainless steel plate—resilient,
indestructible, extremely hygienic
and easy to clean. Finally, in
2000, it happened. In a moment
of grace, with the assistance
of gastronome Alberto Gozzi,
Jasper succeeded where so many
other designers have failed:
a three-dimensional serving dish,
in the most classic old Sheffield
tradition, revisited!

△ *Tin family* (1998) is a family
of stainless steel containers
for storing salt, sugar, cereals,
biscuits and cakes. Morrison
takes the history of design
types forwards once more,
cautiously and bravely taking
small but crucial steps.

▷ In perfect minimalist fine
tuning with the *Tin family*
(2002) presents a series of
Round tray, *Basket*, *Salad
bowl*, *Small cup* and *Ashtray*.

ALESSI

Massimo Morozzi

◁ *Pasta set* is, simply, a homage to pasta. Morozzi showed me the project in 1982. The shape of the object was attractive and yet mysterious. We organized a survey: roughly half of those interviewed did not realize it was a saucepan for boiling water, and came up with all kinds of interpretations. Nevertheless, we decided to manufacture it, and that was a sound decision. *Pasta set* has become so popular that it has had a profound influence on the market, winning the Gold Medal in 1986 at the Ljubljana Bio 11, and spawning at least a hundred imitators the world over. The project continued with *Vapor set* (1990) designed for steam cooking.

▽ Captivated by the whimsical crumpled effect of a silver paper tray, Clotet reproduced the effect in stainless steel (1994).

Lluís Clotet

Alberto Meda

▽ Inspired by the maxim "save energy to stay warm," Meda's *Kalura* hotplate (2001) is an energy-conscious, practical and exceedingly efficient household appliance, designed to minimize electricity use and cut long-term consumption. Just a few minutes after plugging it in, it has accumulated all the energy it needs to keep food warm at the table for an hour. An extremely rare example of a wireless appliance (it comes to the table minus its electricity cable) free from an encumberment common to practically every single household appliance. It is a useful and practical addition to the stage where everyday we play out our convivial moments.

Marc Newson

○ I first heard of Marc in the mid-eighties. Massimo Morozzi met Marc on a triumphant trip to Australia, and came back with a prototype of his first wristwatch, which now has a proud place in the Alessi Museum. Massimo told me that Marc was a very young Australian designer destined, in his opinion, to go a long, long way. Born in 1963, Newson certainly has gone a long way, and is one of the most promising young designers at work today.

◁ The *Gemini* salt mill and pepper mill and, right, the *Stavros* bottle-opener (right, 1999) are fine examples of what I like about his work: his ability to develop his own style, imbued with great originality; in other words, an aptitude for creating striking objects, characterized by a truly innovative form, despite working within a context such as ours in which everything, or practically everything, has already been designed, manufactured, seen and sold.

▷ *"Alberto, it is thrilling to think that Jasper and I will have the chance to become the next Sottsass and Castiglioni of the 2000s..."* This is what Marc said to me when we began working together, so it is not by chance that later he opted to work on the more difficult design types, such as the *Oil, vinegar, salt and pepper cruets* (the project is characterised by surprising ups and downs on the upper part of the shaft) and the *Cheese dish* (2002), so he could pit his skills directly against the great master, Ettore.

ALESSI

△ The *Sygma* clothes-rack and *Titan* soap dish (1999). I find that his forms are extraordinarily faithful to his ideograms, stylistic approach, or whatever you want to call it, characterizing the profound figurative culture of his country. His projects allude to the archetypal forms of aborigine artifacts, as well as objects crafted by nature: for example, bowls hollowed out by the waves of the Australian Ocean, or the colours of certain corals, or tree roots polished smooth by millennia of rain. It is this way of masterfully depicting some of the typical and fundamental characteristics of his homeland, both in a miraculously new fashion, and through simple repetition and copying, that is the most wonderful compliment I could pay him.

◁ *Strelka* (2003) cutlery is an exploit, an extraordinary event in the history of flatware, at least as far as industry production levels are concerned. In fact, this series of items is entirely made with a double asymmetrical surface. A sort of virtuoso production feat, which on one hand gave free rein to the author's well-known sculptural fantasy and on the other hand allows for an unprecedented and surprising balance of the cutlery when gripped.

ALESSI

D'Urbino & Lomazzi

◁ *Augh!* (2000):
Paolo Lomazzi and
Donato D'Urbino,
furniture design
pioneers since the
sixties, have turned their
hands to the extendible
trivet.

▽ An elegant, formal
exercise around the
simplicity of the cup,
the *Double* series
containers (2002), as
the name declares, are
made in a double layer
of stainless steel.

Arnell & Bickford

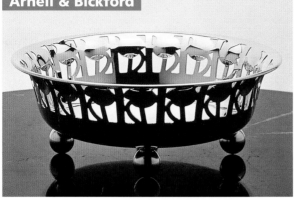

◁ *Rosenschale* is the critical reconstruction of the prototype of a fruit basket designed by Josef Hoffmann in 1906, and never manufactured. Arnell and Bickford worked solely from a photograph —no sketches or drawings have ever been found.

▷ Tools to read and write well by... as computer mice run rampant, Scolari (the name aptly means scholars in Italian!) in 1998 comes up with a *Pencil* in ebonized wood with a lead-tin alloy tip, and a *Paperknife-bookmark*, with two page-marking ribbons, specially designed for people who read books whose pages need cutting.

Massimo Scolari

George Sowden

▽ To soften the invasive finality of a timer's ring, Sowden designed *Alphonse* (1997), an electronic timer which, when the time is up, plays a little tune composed by Steve Piccolo. Which tune it plays depends on the object's colour.

△ Sowden's typical soft, rounded contours and lively colours on his eight function desktop calculator, *Dauphine* (1997).

A L E S S I

Robert Venturi

" What I love about architecture is its complexity and contradiction.
I don't like the incoherence and arbitrary nature of bad architecture, nor the over-elaboration of the picturesque or of expressionism. I love hybrid elements rather than pure ones, the results of compromise rather than cleanliness, the crooked rather than the straight, ambiguity rather than articulation. I prefer richness of meaning to clarity of meaning: I prefer disorder bursting with vitality to obvious single-mindedness: I accept the non-sequitur and proclaim duality. But architecture founded on complexity and contradiction requires a special kind of commitment to the whole. It has to pursue the elusive unity of inclusion, as opposed to the facile unity of exclusion.
More is not less. "

▽ Part of the *Tea & Coffee Piazza* project, *The Campidoglio* tray (1985) echoes Michelangelo's paving in Rome's Capitol Square, highlighting its exceptional perspective shift between the circle and ellipse.

△ *Cuckoo clock* (1988–96) is an amusing challenge for Venturi, coming to grips with a popular genre, very different from *Campidoglio*.

Marco Zanuso

△ The *Duna* range of cutlery (1995) is our sole project by Zanuso, whom I see as something of the Daddy of Italian design. This was designed as a submission to the 1960 competition held by the U.S. firm Reed & Burton; I clearly recall him describing the central element of imagination behind these items as the "narrow life", that is the tapering of the end part of the handle, mirroring the dresses of young ladies from well-to-do fifties families.

Philippe Starck

" Alessi sells joy! "

○ Starck began working with me in 1986, on the French design project *Projet Solférino*, organized together with the Centre Pompidou and François Burkhardt. I cannot help thinking of Starck as the *designer terrible* of our decade. He is a living example of my dream: design, real design, is always highly charged with innovation towards the world of manufacturing and trade, bringing results that need no longer be justified solely on a technological or balance sheet level. A true work of design must move people, convey feelings, bring back memories, surprise, transgress… It must make us feel, intensely, that we are living our one single life… In sum, it has to be poetic. Design is one of the most apt poetic forms of expression of our day. And I know that this great visionary still has plenty of surprises up his sleeve, despite his threats to retire!

△ Starck, "hung" on the hooks of his *Faitoo*. Leader of the French design renaissance, in this brilliant and daring identity photo cum marketing ploy Starck shows he is quick to share the fate of his objects.

◁ A lover of precision instruments (see the *Coo-coo* radio, 1996, right), Starck is also happy to design more commonplace objects, such as this *Dr. Spoon* ear-cleaner, *Dr. Kiss* toothbrush, *Dr. Kleen* toothpick (1998) and *Dr. Cheese* inter-dental brush (1998–99).

◁ The *Hot Bertaa* kettle (1990–97) is skewered by its handle-spout. During the design stage, its compact, almost sacred appearance was shrouded in an aura of mysticism: in his preliminary sketches Starck had penned a Latin inscription around its base.

▷ With the *Boaat* (1998) series, a range of kitchen containers with lids and bowls with feet, Starck continues his research into archetypal eating objects, this time drawing inspiration from Japanese cuisine.

◁ Starck's *Wall Clock* takes up a favourite motif: he liberates the clock hands from their imprisonment, freeing them to roam through space. The clock is made up only of the two hands and its workings: you tell the time from the shadows on the wall, much like a sundial (1990).

△ Starck's projects have, in time, assumed the name and appearance of animate presences in the domestic environment: here we have the *Max-le-Chinois* colander and the suggestive, mysterious, leggy *Juicy Salif* lemon squeezer, both from 1990. To celebrate this item, without doubt Starck's best-known design for Alessi—it had its tenth anniversary in 2000 —we brought out a special gold-plated limited edition. This version, as the instructions advise, is best not used but displayed on your bookshelves.

△ *Faitoo*, "fait-tout," came out in 1996. In French it means both "do-it-all" and saucepan. It is a long bar to hang in the kitchen, with hooks for hanging all kinds of things by their handles or through special holes. Everything is visible and within reach, spelling an end to those frustrating "where can it be?" moments in the kitchen.

△ *Voilà Voilà*: the tray rushes along on its little green feet (1992).

△ The *Cake Server* looks as solid and manoeuvrable as a bricklayer's trowel (1998).

△ The unmistakable silhouette of *Mister Meumeu* conceals a parmesan cheese cellar with grater: the horn is in actual fact, a spoon (1992) .

▽ The gleaming surface of the *Centre-piece* is supported by "attendants": barely sketched grey or orange characters redolent of Starck's recent "anthropomorphic" works (1996).

◁ Starck's output spans precision mechanisms (such as the clocks or the radio) and seemingly everyday objects, such as the *Dr. Skud* fly swatter which, when moved, reveals a human face (1998).

△ In 1996 we acquired Starck's and Patricia's small company, adding several articles to our catalogue including the *O'Kelvin* candlestick (1989), *Joe Cactus* ashtray (1990) and *Berta Youssouf* place-holder (1987).

WELCOME

△ The chubby, solitary *Dédé* meditates on his soft aluminium rotundities and on his role as a doorstop (1996).

Dédé
design Philippe Starck, (1994) 1996

ALESSI

Enzo Mari

" *Italian design manufacturers are, in actual fact, metaphors for manufacturers.* "

○ Enzo Mari harbours towards the consumer society a critical attitude that is beyond compare on the international design scene, despite the latter is so multifarious. Without question he is my "master of paranoia": a sort of guardian angel on my shoulder who wags a disapproving finger when I do something he feels I shouldn't! We met in the late seventies, when I wanted to include his *Arran* tray, designed for Danese, in our *Programme 7* —and I succeeded, finally, twenty years later, in 1997. In a conference held in Paris, with his characteristic verbal vehemence, he expressed the concept I have cited above. The words struck me, I made them mine, and the sentence has served as a launchpad for theoretical research into the "Factories of Italian Design." I am delighted he is still working and building up his family in our catalogue. I find his criticisms valuable; every now and then we need him to reset the needle of our compass to North, the direction it should be pointing in, even in mid-storm.

△ *Ecolo* is Mari's most emblematic project: turning discarded plastic bottles into vases for flowers (1996).

◁ The *Standard* two-level three-wheeled trolley (1989) was Mari's first Alessi project. Designed to be one of the furnishing accessories for my "House of Happiness," it is extremely solid and manoeuvrable: features that make it suited to professional as well as home use.

▽ The *Arran* (1961) rectangular tray, originally designed for Danese, became one of the most significant Italian design projects of the sixties, as well as an archetype in the history of this object. It has been on our catalogue since 1997.

▽ Reproductions of several classic Mari designs for Danese from the fifties and sixties. We acquired the rights and put them back into production in 1997.

ALESSI

◁ To my mind, Mari is the greatest proponent of the "stripped-down" approach to design applied to industrial manufacturing: he refrains from the temptations of allowing his fantasy to run wild, so no gratuitous frills creep into his designs just to please the public (he refers to them as *cazzettini*, polite translation of which approximates to rubbish"). His is just a constant quest for the archetypal simplicity that, on its own, should justify the birth of a new object into our already overcrowded consumer society. An example is this citrus-fruit squeezer (stoically named *Titanic*), in which he inventively tackles and succeeds with all those minor details that have made previous citrus squeezers unpleasant and sometimes impractical. Not just lovely to look at, it's lightweight and hard-wearing, highly practical, easy and fun to use—in sum, a little masterpiece in its own right, even though its subtlety has sometimes meant that it has had a hard time standing out in the bewildering and crowded landscape of household products…

◁ The so-called Mari family of *Strainers and Colanders* (1997), now available in new colours.

▷ The *Kitchen box for salt etc.*, made out of translucent plastic, takes up the sometimes delicate topic of the hinge, a popular element in many sixties designs. This interpretation comes up with a brilliant design innovation— the box and lid hook together without needing any intermediate element (1999).

Twergi and Tendentse

▽ These pages present the "historical" utensils made by Ubaldo Piazza in the thirties, interspersed with contemporary objects.

Twergi

○ The other deep-rooted manufacturing tradition in the Strona valley, apart from metals, consists in small wooden items for home and kitchen. In our desire to return to these roots, in 1988 we took over the valley's oldest original firm, Battista Piazza 1865. We have reproduced a number of historical items from the first few decades of this century, and revitalized the working of wood: our own designers and many young people have come up with a host of projects using many kinds of wood. In 1998 the company was incorporated by Alessi.

△ The output of the Piazza firm represented the industrial evolution of local crafts. The little elf, known as "twergi" in the Walser dialect, is the historic symbol of that. The good-natured little woodland sprite has been redesigned by Milton Glaser, who has set him on a tiny pair of skis.

ALESSI

△ Andrea Branzi has found that wood is a material suited to his poetic style, and over the years he has designed several of Twergi's best projects.

▷ Twergi was a training ground for young designers: Enrico Marforio, David Rooz, Berto Pandolfo, Paolo Pagani, Walter Conti, Sophie Suchodolski, Bortolani and Becchelli, Pozzoli and Ribet, Paolo Grasselli, Yvan von Allmen, Animal Design… Right, the *Mirror* by Migliore and Servetto (1992–98), Glaser's *Lamp* (1989–97): and *Photo Holders* by Kuno Prey (1990).

▽ Ettore Sottsass fell in love with the *Twergi* wood designing as well as coordinating projects by his young assistants.

○ Tendentse was set up in Livorno in 1995 as a small-article manufacturer, principally experimenting with new departures in majolica and porcelain. The first collection included works by Branzi, Cibic, De Lucchi, Gili, Mendini, Morozzi, Mutoh, Nannetti, Nardi, Natalini,

Tendentse

Puppa, Raggi, Shama, Tarshito and Sottsass, today all out of production. Since 1989 Tendentse has been part of Alessi.

ALESSI

100% Make Up

○ The metaproject of this venture, overseen by Alessandro Mendini, is the production of an ideal aesthetic factory, understood as a multiplication of individuals, as a sequence of aesthetic creatures all resembling one another. To obtain difference from the identical, one hundred authors worked on a single starting shape: in 1992 each finished article was produced in a run of 100, numbered from 1 to 10,000 and signed by all the designers at the same time.

❝ *The decorations are like fishes in the sea: they exist even if you can't see them.* **❞**

△ My brother Michele, our general manager, surrounded by just a few of the one hundred vases (1992).

△ Mendini designed the standard gold-coloured vase (number 58 in the series), as well as various other possible decorations and stagings of the hundred vases, drawing ironic inspiration from various sequences or display possibilities.

TIPO PARATA MILITARE

△ 1) Antonio Abate 2) Carla Accardi 3) Sanchita Ajjampur 4) Yael Applefeld
5) Quinuajuaq Ashewak 6) Paolo Bertozzi and Stefano Del Monte Casoni
7) Gabriel Bien-Aimé 8) Lapo Binazzi 9) Alighiero Boetti 10) Andreas Brandolini
11) Frédéric Bruly Bouabré 12) Sergio Calatroni 13) Juli Capella
14) Sergio Cappelli and Patrizia Ranzo 15) Nigel Coates 16) Cocktail
17) Gianni Colombo 18) Riccardo Dalisi 19) Nicola De Maria 20) Jan Digerud.

△ 21) Emmanuel Ekefrey 22) Brian Eno 23) Ellinor Flor 24) Dan Friedman 25) Elizabeth Fritsch
26) Piero Gaeta 27) Giorgio Galli and Beatrice Santiccioli 28) Louise Gibb 29) Piero Gilardi
30) Anna Gili 31) Milton Glaser 32) Michael Graves 33) Maria Christina Hamel
34) Jan Mohamed Hanif 35) Pitt Heinke 36) Yoshiki Hishinuma 37) Susan Holm
38) Yong Ping Huang 39) Aussi Jaffari 40) Christer Jonson.

◁ 41) Bodys Isek
Kingelez
42) Inka Kivalo
43) Mark Kostabi
44) Randi
Kristensen
45) Milan Kunc
46) Kunstflug
47) Shiro
Kuramata
48) Quim Larrea
49) Cheikh Ledy
50) Stefan
Lindfors.

ALESSI

△ 51) Kamba Luesa 52) Esther Mahlangu 53) Valente Malangatana
54) Karel Malich 55) Massimo Mariani 56) Giusi Mastro 57) Kivuthi Mbuno
58) Alessandro Mendini 59) Antonio Miralda 60) Sergei Vladimir Mironenko
61) Alexandre Mocika 62) Paola Navone 63) Sinya Okayama 64) Luigi Ontani
65) Eikki Orvola 66) Salcido Javier Perez-Gil 67) Eduardo Pla 68) Plumcake
69) Giorgio Rava 70) Ravage.

△ 71) Ronaldo Pereira Rego 72) Roberto Remi 73) Cheri Samba 74) Andreas Schulze
75) Suresh Sethi 76) Raja Babu Sharma 77) Jari Silvennoinen 78) Ettore Sottsass, Jr.
79) Gregorio Spini 80) Philippe Starck 81) Peter Struycken 82) Sybilla 83) Guillermo Tejeda
84) Cyprien Tokoudagba 85) Dagmar Trinks 86) Maurizio Turchet 87) Twins Seven Seven
88) Masanori Umeda 89) Hilde Vemren 90) Robert Venturi.

▷ 91) Guido
Venturini
92) Nanda Vigo
93) Mara Voce
94) Acharya Vyakul
95) Brigitta Watz
96) Gisbert Weiss
97) Hannes
Wettstein
98) Y.A. Y.A. Young
Aspirations Young
Artists
99) Leonid Yentus
100) Rhonda
Zwillinger.

King-Kong Family

" We've had enough of erudite designers like Mendini or Branzi, you need to have a degree in architecture to understand their designs… We'd like to design things that appeal to Leo Castelli and to ordinary folk too. "

○ In the late eighties, in his usual discreet manner Alessandro Mendini—an invaluable conduit of new talents—told me of two young architects from Florence. Stefano Giovannoni and Guido Venturini came to see me, very nervous, with some sketches. They were two rather odd-looking guys, and I felt that their playful and elementary poetics, often closely inspired by the formal style of cartoons, was full of potential. I had them shown around the factory and did my best to fill them in about us, our hopes and possibilities. They listened to me very attentively, and the next time they came back with a whole book crammed with design notes.

▷ Among their drawings I found a very straightforward tray, its edge perforated with a little man motif, like the ones children cut out with scissors. The *Girotondo* project (1989) went ahead without any particular hitches or special enthusiasm: nobody could have imagined this would become our best-selling tray!

Those little King-Kong "men" have turned up on the edging of objects that belong to the most consolidated Alessi tradition, such as our *Trays* or *Baskets*. Now, though, they have multiplied and have set out to invade familiar territories (such as the chopping board, napkin holder or photo holder) and unfamiliar ones (keyring, bookmark, candles). Their apotheosis, though, has to be *Girotondo* (Ring-around-the-rosy) *Jewellery* (1998).

To be honest, I think that the King-Kongs, despite their indubitable intuition and great flair, have been lucky too. They were spot on with the "playful style," they understood how important it is to work with "emotional codes," but above all the project came at the right time, and its place in the Alessi catalogue hit the spot.

With hindsight, I'd say it was a typical case of applying the "child code" to a catalogue like ours, until then dominated by the authority, status and *style* of great designers' masterpieces: a counterweight to the then emerging talents of Rossi, Graves and Starck.

▷ Alongside the expanding family of "little men," since 1994 we have also produced a range of *Baskets*, *Fruit Bowls*, *Trays* and *Breadstick Holders* of varying sizes, all perforated with a triangle and rhomboid motif.

ALESSI

CSA and Young Designers

LAURA

○ The Centro Studi Alessi (CSA) was set up in 1990 for two purposes: to draw up theoretical papers on topics associated with objects (to be then published as books), and to coordinate the work I was willing to start with young designers. Up until that time Alessi had only worked with "major designers," and I felt a certain degree of responsibility towards young, upcoming designers. Laura Polinoro, whom Mendini suggested, has done valuable work.

❝ It is not easy to describe this 'workshop': fertile, subtle, a place where, like in a fairytale everything seems possible, where you cannot see a beginning nor know how it will all end… ❞

▷ The pictures on this page are taken from a workshop held at the Helsinki University of Industrial and Applied Art in 1996 and in Tokyo in 1997.

Laura has brought to Alessi the intuition and semiological training garnered at the school of Eco and Fabbri. She sometimes reminds me of Marianne Brandt, the first woman to work at the Bauhaus Metallwerkstatt during the twenties. Laura started the arduous process of shaking Alessi out of its contentedness with a rethorical heritage typical of certain high-flown Italian design. Through her we have brought new disciplines to Alessi, anthropology and semiology to name but two. Nine years on, in 1998, the CSA moved from Milan to Crusinallo.

◁ The CSA's design management work takes place principally through workshops and design seminars with students, in collaboration with architecture faculties and schools of art and design, as well as with groups of specially invited designers. We have held workshops all over the world: in Argentina, England, Japan, Brazil, Costa Rica, the U.S., Australia, France, Germany, Finland, Austria, Korea and even in the Aegean Islands.

ALESSI

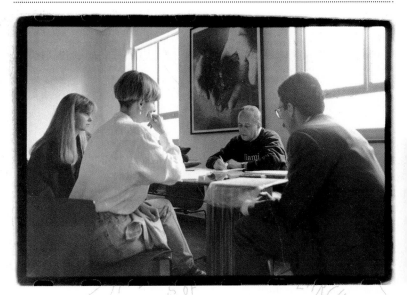

In 1990 I too was entrusted with this task, which I undertake with great enthusiasm: these photographs show the workshop held at Miami University in 1996. Each year I do my best to set aside at least two periods to hold personal workshops. I have taken great pleasure in trying to teach young people about my field, and I'm curious to find out what they think about us, how they consider what Alessi is doing. The workshops are not just about teaching, they also play a significant operational role, sometimes leading to veritable projects, and verifying the suitability of designs for manufacture. To sum up, it's a very interesting part of Alessi's open policy towards the concept of "metaproject," the creation of a structure of ongoing mental research.

▷ In more recent years our workshop activity
has no longer been undertaken just by Laura
and by myself: new figures have emerged
in Alessi, including Kristiina Lassus and Gloria
Barcellini, who have actually organised and
managed much of the work in my stead.
From top to bottom, the four photos refer
to the project by Olga Szablewicz (*Madonna*
salt and pepper pots) developed by the Sztuk
Pieknych Academy of Warsaw in 2000,
to a project by Sebastian Liedtke

(the *Jelly* cup/freshener) developed by
Bremerhaven's Design Labor during a
workshop conducted with Gijs Bakker in 1999,
and to projects by Hubert Gasthaus (*Armed
Candlestick*) and Lothar Windels (the *Fritz*
trolley), both created during a workshop
held with Ron Arad, Sebastian Bergne
and Konstantin Grcic at the Royal College
of Art in London (1999).

ALESSI

Memory Containers Creole Project

○ The first metaproject coordinated by CSA, it meant opening up Alessi to young designers; actually, to be precise, young women designers, as during the introductory phase around 200 women designers under 30 were invited from all over the world. The questions we were asking: what is expected of the object? How are objects born, how do they change when moving from one culture to another? What changes in their shape, perception, use? How does an object become a cultural object?
This was an exploration into the archetypes of presentation and "offering" of food and its rituals, with inspiration coming from the memory of a culture or a personal experience. The goal was to realize a "Creole" project, a test-tube cloning of that which, given its natural span, happens much more slowly when different cultures come together.

△ After several years of severe segregation, Memory Containers was then accessed by some of the young male designers: *Spice Tower* was created by the German Wolfgang Hints (2000).

△ The *Chimu* table centrepiece bowl by English designer Joanna Lyle (1992).

◁ *Win*, the bossed glass, by Italian designer Anna Gili (1994).

△ Pierced *Basket* by Australian designer Susan Cohn (1992), also responsible for the *Cohndom Box* on the right (1999), the elegant and provocative holder for condoms.

◁ The *Brasero* (1992): Pampas lamp-chafing dish, by the Argentinean Maria Sanchez.

▽ The form of the *Uma* (2002) incense-burner is inspired by strong symbolism: in many cultures the Egg is the symbol of both a microcosm and of the Great Universe, of fertility and creativity, the genesis of all things, of the male/female relationship. In turn, the Plate symbolizes offering and the choice of black represents the Universe.

▽ After several decades of silence, three kitchen containers *Kalistò* by English designer Clare Brass (1992) marked the revival of an item much seen in early Alessi catalogues.

◁ Couscous is a tasty dish, but more importantly it is an ancient ritual in Mediterranean African countries and also one of the world's most popular foods. The Algerian designer Abdi Abdelkader has created his *Couscoussière* and the great *Gsâa* large ceramic container (1999).

ALESSI

◁ *Cactus* bowl by Marta Sansoni (2002). Fretwork as a theme can be found in an extensive range of decoration, which since its origins accompanies the history of man. The use of fretwork became particularly interesting in the industrial era, namely from 1850s onwards, when the application of stylized naturalistic decorative motifs was used to endow early industrial products with greater dignity. Over the decades the Alessi catalogues have brought new variations on this theme.

△ The Iranian designer Khodi Feiz: *Salsa* (2000) is not only for serving the Mexican dish from which it takes its name, but also goes divinely with crudités or any little hors d'oeuvre tidbits.

▷ The *Helmut* citrus-fruit holder by Cecilia Cassina (1992) and the large *Tralcio muto* tray by Marta Sansoni (2000, left): other two examples of our expertise in cold metalworking.

▽ Large oval bowl
Amfitheatrof (2000), *Uni* soap
holder and *Unicci* toothbrush
holder (2003) by Francesca
Amfitheatrof.

Memory Containers
Biological Project

spezie in polvere

le foglie

◁ The relationship between steel and glass looms large in the Biological Project. Left, Pierangelo Caramia's *Biscuit box* and Theo Williams's *Honey pot* (1995). Below, Joanna Lyle's *Kitchen boxes,* and bottom, Alejandro Ruiz's *Parmenides* parmesan cheese grater (1994). Above, the *Oggetto dell'equilibrio* (1996) is a set for perfuming and restoring balance to the home.

○ This chapter examines a new vein of research: the discovery of Es, as a primary concept of perception, more closely associated with intuition and receptive capabilities than the expression of different cultures through stylistic languages. The goal is to unearth new relationships linking the rule and the project: the living, vital object wins the man and nature conflict.

F.F.F. Family Follows Fiction

○ The metaproject F.F.F., begun in 1991, grew out of a desire to explore the emotional structure of objects even more profoundly than we had done in the past. We were interested in the most delicate, intimate, sensory human needs. The objects became ludic tools, telling little tales, giving captivating twists to everyday uses, suggesting a mediation with playfulness… they become a bridge to the fantastical.

▷ Biagio Cisotti's funny little devil bottle-openers, *Diabolix* (1994) are still one of F.F.F.'s most popular items.

◁ The coloured resin version (1993) of Christopher Dresser's historic sugar bowl with feet (1864).

◁ Mattia Di Rosa's laughing little creatures (the *Gianni* containers, 1994, the *Bimboveloce* cakestand, 1996 and, on the next page, *Carlo* the bottle cap, 1994). He is the youngest designer in the catalogue.

ALESSI

▽ *Miamor*, a portrait frame/message holder with a secret compartment by Enrica Zanzi (1996).

For F.F.F. we drew upon Winnicott's words on "transitional objects," as well as Franco Fornari's theory of "emotional codes." At the outset the idea was to reproduce the process of creation and animation of the object common to the world of childhood and to primitive cultures.

◁ *Pig Pencil* (2002), Massimo Giacon's pencil sharpener.

◁ Once again by Miriam, the first object in the brand new series, *Montagna dei Cani*, dedicated to our four-legged friends: *Lupita* (2002).

▽ *Häagen Dazs* by Miriam Mirri (2002), is a large ice-cream dish for lovers (in the dual sense), complete with a large, special spoon. The item was developed in collaboration with Häagen Dazs themselves and I must make mention of the special commitment dedicated to this project by Danilo Alliata, my priceless design assistant who, amongst other things, has an inordinate passion for ice-cream.

▽ *Match* by Roderick Vos and Henco Penzy (2002): piezoelectric lighter that lights up on its own when the arm moves down towards the gas ring.

▽ Stefano Pirovano pursues his research into playful little sensorial design performances with his *Peppino* pepper grinder, *Salo* salt mill and *Te ò* (2000) tea strainer.

▷ *Marcel* (2002), a wall-mount magazine rack by WAAC's.

○ As well as the kitchen, which in the last twenty years has provided food for thought for the vast majority of our designs, another part of the house, the bathroom, has gradually become one of the most intriguing growth areas for people's domestic fantasy. It is interesting that this phenomenon has developed without manufacturers having too much to do with it: very few bathroom objects, large or small, express really interesting, fun, poetic design. A few years ago we began to fill this gap.

▽ With a burgeoning family of bright characters in thermoplastic rubber—*Rondo* cap for toothpaste tube, *Otto* interdental thread holder and *Sden* toothbrush cover (1998)—Stefano Pirovano has set his sights on bringing some fun to dental hygiene for children (and adults too).

Mr. Suicide

▽ A cartoonist by profession, a man of talent and great personality, Massimo Giacon has turned his narrative abilities and usual whimsy to designing the *Mr. Cold* liquid soap dispenser and *Mr. Suicide* bathplug (2000) and *Anubis* container (2001).

As well as the limited number of designs dedicated to the bathroom, featured under their individual designers, this page illustrates several playful new designs.

▷ The soap dish *Vanity* (1999) by Antonio Cagianelli: a new designer goes with a name that is also an aesthetic programme…

Stefano Giovannoni

" But who is this Michael Graves? He's certainly not a designer! "

○ A "born again" designer par excellence, bearing a vague resemblance to a rumpled teddy bear, a man who looks like he might be anything except a much-acclaimed designer, Stefano conceals one of the most explosive talents I have ever had the good fortune to come across. He is not happy to be classified as "one of the young," he feels he is destined for the designer hall of fame, and he wants to have his share of acclaim with my "masters." He'll no doubt get there, even if a little grizzly and impatient at times.

◁ The *Mary biscuit* boxes (1995) speak a soft, flowing language: with such sweet and soft dispositions, I am convinced that all Giovannoni's objects look at us affectionately with the mysterious yet warm smile of the *Mona Lisa*, "...that smile associated with the sentiment of beauty which in adulthood moves the human heart, which for all of us, when falling in love or glimpsing a beautiful thing, is apparently associated with the intense visual relationship established with our mother's face, constituted as representative of the intra-uterine bliss" (Frontori, 1986).

◁ *Lilliput* (1993) is Giovannoni's highly original and inventive salt and pepper set. The two containers have magnetic feet which stick to the base.

▷ "Macaroni, you've pushed me to the limit and now I'm going to eat you!" This is how Italian comic Alberto Sordi enjoined battle with a huge plate of steaming pasta. *Rigatone* is an invitation to eat Mediterranean-style, a kitchen box for spaghetti designed by Giovannoni (1998), whose shape and "topping" (a tomato lid) mimic what is probably Italy's best-known dish.

△ *Gnam*: a cartoon-character name for the bread bin designed by Giovannoni in 2000. The cartoon inspiration is evident in the simple river pebble form, and in the extraordinary, brilliant transparency of the materials employed.

△ *Happy Spices* is a family of containers and dispensers for spices, salt and pepper (1997).

◁ *Fruit Mama*: is it a big, welcoming hand holding up the fruit, or a "new apple tree"? Definitely another non-anonymous presence in the house, which Giovannoni wishes to animate with a thousand characters of all kinds (1993).

▽ Mnemonic references are easy for the *Rimini* cutlery drainer (1998). The visual pointer is explicit and heart-warming: that old bucket abandoned so many times on a beach with its spade and sand moulds.

△ *Flute* (2002): it is said that flowers must be one and a half times the height of the container being used, but in this design the classic proportion ratio cannot be applied. This vase looks good not only with poppies, but also with a "swallowed" rose (where only the blossom emerges from the vase) or with a longer stem, but in any case stripped of all its leaves.

▽ *Spank* (2000) reminds us of a classic estrangement trick: an everyday object changes its dimensions and subverts its proportions, leaving its usual function. In this case, a children's game has become a carpet beater.

▽ *Superpepper* (2003), the vegetable grinder: another brilliant example of the use of metaphor in a playful vein, of which Giovannoni is the recognized precursor.

ALESSI

▷ Ex-children may recall a small and well-loved cartoon character called Grisù, a little dragon always busy trying to remedy the damage caused by the fire he inadvertently breathes. We trust that those who get to grips with the long neck of this diminutive household dragon *Bruce*, will be more careful with this hot item, a table lighter (1998).

△ *Cico* (2000) is another very recent example of Stefano's more figurative, anthropomorphic and zoomorphic narrative approach.

△ Toothpicks may be indispensable, but they can be embarrassing to use: to put a light touch to what is not a particularly refined gesture, Giovannoni pulls out a rabbit from the unpredictable top hat of his creativity: the *Magic Bunny* toothpick holder (1998).

◁ In 2002 the cheeky little rabbit makes a comeback as a kitchen-roll holder in *Bunny & Carrot*.

▷ *Ship Shape* (1998) is a creative container: it can be used for sauces, butter, jams… Sweet or savoury, it comes with a ready-to-use spatula for your imaginative delights.

▽ An international character with a long-standing pedigree in texts on pedagogy and psychoanalysis, Pinocchio is now a long-nosed funnel, the smiling *Pino* (1998): truth or lie?

△ The *Nutty the Cracker* nutcracker (1993) is an example of how Giovannoni works, his finger on the pulse of our emotional codes, in particular that of the mother and child.

▽ Among so many festive eating rites, there is one lonely and melancholic pastime: breaking into a boiled egg, an act which is usually performed in reluctant intimacy, in a deep silence broken only by those tentative blows to the shell, making the humble boiled egg almost a metaphor for crepuscular solitude. Giovannoni has managed to brighten this moment up, to make it a playful and gregarious thing with *Coccodandy* (1998), his basket for cooking eggs, which comes with four highly coloured recesses for cooking and serving eggs to friends.

△ Electric torch, *Flash* (2001), developed in collaboration with Flos.

ALESSI

▷ The cartoon effect reaches its apogee with the infamous *Merdolino* (1993). Without any reticence, Giovannoni tackles an indispensable but "taboo" object, the toilet brush, turning it into a slender vase from which sprouts a long, allusive and inviting shrub.

◁ The latest addition to the bathroom for the time being is the natural rubber hot water bottle, *Hot Bott* (2001).

▷ A few years on from the now-legendary *Merdolino*, which shocked the conventional stalwarts of design, Stefano has struck again at the same target—there's no more delicate way of putting it. His *Johnny the Diver* plunger (1999), soapdish and *Big Bubbles* toothbrush holder cup (1999) and the *Up-pill* make-up remover pad dispenser (2001) all confirm his vocation and interest in this area of the home that has all too often been ignored by design.

Mami

▷ *Mami* (1999–2001) is the third set of saucepans
in the history of Alessi, after *La Cintura di Orione*
by Sapper and *Falstaf* by Mendini. This time I
entrusted to a young designer the difficult task of
stimulating people's imagination by exploring the
archaic world of "kitchenware." The spelt soup
bubbles once again in the earthenware jar, and
the capacious, rotund and sacred pots "with two
ears" (as Catullus wrote) evoke the warmth of
bygone eras. The truly complete set, in total
harmony with Giovannoni's "poetics of the
emotions," also includes the frying pans and
beafsteak pans in non-stick cast aluminium.

La pentola
Mami
1999
Stefano Giovannoni

Alessi. Extra ordinary.

Milano Strasbourg Hamburg Stockholm Oslo Helsinki Tokyo Singapore

ALESSI

△ It is no secret that a pressure cooker (a device invented by Denis Papin in 1679) was lacking from the catalogue of a metal household objects manufacturer, which is what we continue to be, at least in name. And we have actually been thinking about it for a while and discussing it with several designers. *Mami* (2003) pressure cooker: several years have passed since the start of the design project and I think that Stefano and my technicians have done an excellent job and met the challenge of creating a pressure cooker worthy of being called an Alessi. They acted carefully and with expertise in order to produce an item that is particularly delicate and complex from a technical and functional standpoint. They were able to create a sophisticated and technologically evolved cooking tool that is, at long last, "beautiful," in an environment that seemed doomed to loiter in a relentless mood of sloppy ungainliness.

▽ *Pasta set* (2001) and *Milk skimmer* (2002).

▷ Alessi completes its vision of fundamental tableware items with this range of *Mami* (2003) porcelain tea service and series of glasses, generated by a designer whose singular mix of expressive talent, humor and understanding of consumer mentality was a hallmark of the 1990s. However, the whole *Mami* family marks a turning point in Giovannoni's poetry: embarking on a new route that I am tempted to define as the quest for classicism, harmony and archetype, stated in the coded matrix that he has mastered. Watch out for it.

▷ *Fruitscape* (2003)

▷ The *Mami* cutlery service (2002).

▽ The *Mami* series continues through 2002, with kitchen knives.

STEFANO GIOVANNONI

Ethno

▽ *Ethno* (2000), conceived
to be the new pop icon of the
twenty-first century, has been
made into objects from our
most classic metal—stainless
steel—with finely decorative
results, and become a plastic
range too (transmuted into
neo-industrial North African
items).

Guido Venturini

" *Fields of expression such as art, music and cinema allow you to get out the nasty, ugly, violent things, though they provide a release because of their very nature. Design does not usually offer such opportunities...* "

○ Guido is a committed explorer of the "twilight zone." His objects are highly expressive characters: wild, certainly out of the ordinary, vaguely monstrous but never threatening, on the contrary to me they look like they're asking for our assistance. Guido does a lot of thinking about the role of the designer in today's society, he is aware of the contradictions inherent in our work: I like seeing his work as that of a conscientious objector. Good old Guido, we'll travel far together, as long as you don't get lost along the way!

▽ This gas lighter is called *Firebird* (1993), but the name is not a homage to Stravinsky. It is one of the most explicit and "courageous" of all the characters in the Alessi catalogue, an ironic reference to the "erotic code."

◁ The *Nonno di Antonio* garlic squeezer.

▽ The china dishes, crystal glasses and steel and plastic cutlery of this complete *Dinner Service* make it the centrepiece of Guido's production. As is sometimes the case with our more complex projects, the gestation period for this one was long: six years of work. The results show the wait was worth it—once again, unmistakably, we are treated to the underlying theme of Venturini's poetics: the anthropomorphic and fetishistic iconography that hints at the "dark side," with the elegantly neo-primitive stylistic cues.

▷ PIctured below: *Yong* cutlery, *Pluto* porcelain and *Porthos* and *Acqua* glasses (2001) To the right, porcelain with new *Hikuri* decoration (2002).

▽ *Mangiauovo* (2001), a design from a concept by Genoese inventors Terrile and Marinelli, allowing the egg to be lowered into the saucepan, removed when ready and eaten.

◁ The *Fred Worm* vacuum bottle (1997). Guido's designs are so anthropomorphic and powerful that once we received an e-mail from Dallas, Texas, from a certain Fred Worm who asked us to pay him a royalty for using his name…

▷ *Gino Zucchino* (1993) a sugar sifter, but at Alessi it has become so popular it has turned into a kind of garden gnome.

△ *Inka* press filter coffee maker (2000). As with the cutlery, our designer and technicians have really applied themselves to using the latest plastics in an innovative way, drawing upon the extraordinary functional and sensorial qualities of this material—which remain evident as long as it is not used in too "cheap" a way, so often the case with mass-produced household goods.

▷ *Super G.* lamp: a lighting fetish made with rotating technique (2001).

▷ Faithful to his creative
exploration of the shadowy
corners of the unconscious,
after a long gestation (due
mainly to a lengthy sojourn
in the Mexican desert), spring
2000 sees the birth of two
more characters, the *Okkio!*
table brush for removing
crumbs and clothes brush
for removing fluff.

◁ The *Antonio* coat hanger
(1996) was one of Alessi's
first non self-standing objects,
designed to be affixed to a
wall. In 2000 it was joined by
its brother *Antonio C*, a toilet
roll holder. The family grows
in 2001 with the *Antonio A*
towel rail, *Antonio S* soapdish
and *Antonio D* toothbrush
holder.

▷ The very well-built
Antonio shows off his
powerful muscles
in a body-building
clothes hook.

Historical Reproductions

Anonimo Pompeiano

○ When reviewing the history of the applied arts, especially that of smaller household articles, I never cease to be amazed by the substantial invariability of standard models: a goblet, a tray or a spoon are the fruit of an ongoing virtual work in progress conducted by a few hundred designers—mostly unknown—over thousands of years of human history. Almost all the objects we deal in have ancient origins, and are strongly conditioned by rituals, plucked either from memory or the collective unconscious. We present some of these past designs in this chapter, illustrating creative moments, historical epochs and prototypes by major creators in our own specific field.

▽ With the aid of Neapolitan architects and archaeologists, in 1997 we reconstructed a scale model steel tray for this small first-century A.D. Roman bronze sculpture of a jester/focaccia hawker, found at the *House of Ephebus* at Pompeii, kept at the Naples Archaeological Museum.

▷ A leading figure in the shift to the modern in Finnish objects and architecture, Eliel Saarinen (1873–1950) had an organic and unitary vision of design: using plain geometric shapes (suited, incidentally, to industrial processing) Saarinen broke a great deal of new ground with the concept of "domestic landscape."
This silver *Tea set with urn*, that we produced in 1987, is considered one of the archetypes of American design.

Eliel Saarinen

Piero Bottoni

◁ The *Modular element candies bowl* (1991), designed around 1928 is an exemplary Piero Bottoni piece: elegant rationalism, in no way self-satisfied, displaying clear classic lines yet totally practical. It is very interesting to see an object made up of a cone and circle mutate into a living shape through the arrangement of its components.

ALESSI

Christopher Dresser

△ Dresser's many silver objects (the *Teapots*, the *Cruet sets*, the *Parmesan cheese-butter bowl with ice holder*) show he was always far ahead of his time.

○ Dresser (1834–1904) was an illustrious English botanist and scholar of the decorative arts who was probably the first industrial designer in the modern sense of the term. Unlike his Arts & Crafts Movement contemporaries, he wholeheartedly accepted all the implications of industrial mass-production, harnessing this to the design of bold, highly visionary crafted objects.

▷ This *Toast-rack* (1878), manufactured in stainless steel in 1991, has functional lines that are a foretaste of the Bauhaus spirit.

△ Dresser was a prime example of the "Moderate Transgression" I seek in design. His projects show that he knew the techniques of metal production better than any designer who has come to Alessi, and it is no coincidence that some of the objects we have chosen to "reproduce" are naturally suitable to be manufactured in modern day stainless steel.

This did not prevent him from never accepting technique as a goal; he constantly probed boundaries as he sought higher expressive and constructive results. Some of these, such as his *Triangular Teapot* with legs (designed in 1880 and produced in 1991), are even unsettling, while others show daring levels of intellectual and professional openness.

Staatliches Bauhaus

○ Founded by Walter Gropius in Weimar in 1919 as a school of art and applied arts, subsequently directed by Hannes Meyer and Mies van der Rohe, Bauhaus is one of the historic workshops whose *mission* Alessi hopes to share. The reproductions on these pages are by Hans Przyrembel, Marianne Brandt, Otto Rittweger and Josef Knau. Because of the great talents of the people involved, because of its stated desire to develop a practice founded on the principle "Art and Technique: a new unity" at the very moment the problem of reproducing works of art was a passionate topic of debate, because of the obstacles thrown up by conservative opponents and later by Nazism, Bauhaus was one of the legendary originators of the Modern Movement in architecture and design.

▷ The designs shown on these pages were created at the Bauhaus Metallwerkstatt between 1924 and 1930, prevalently under the tutelage of Lazló Moholy-Nagy (seen here with Marianne Brandt). They are manufactured under license from the Bauhaus Archiv in Berlin. On the facing page, the sleek *Tea doser* (Hans Przyrembel, 1926), *Sugar and creamer set* (Marianne Brandt and Helmut Schulze, 1926), and the *Set of two tea infusers* (Otto Rittweger and Josef Knau, 1924), all from 1995. In the middle, the *Tea and coffee service* (Marianne Brandt, 1924), manufactured in 1985.

▽ In a photo self-portrait which has become famous, Marianne Brandt, who made all the works on this page, "wears" metal items as if they were jewels.

ALESSI

Josef Hoffmann

○ I think that if I had to pick just one designer out of the last century, it would have to be Josef Hoffmann. He founded the Wiener Werkstätte (1903) and left behind an immense body of work of extraordinary innovation, which has influenced generations of designers. That's not all: he was the first practitioner of a new way of working, in which the designer doesn't work *for* but *with* an entrepreneur, influencing and inspiring his ventures, which has become the cornerstone of "Italy's design factories."

△ At last, after all this time, Alessi finally has a "catering" design item! The *Rundes Modell* cutlery set, created in 1906 and manufactured by Alessi in 2000 under licence from the Österreichisches Museum für Angewandte Kunst, was originally conceived for the legendary Cabaret Fledermaus in Vienna: a public place, a cabaret, a restaurant, really. Not just any old nightspot, though; it is not hard to imagine Schindler, Mahler, Schiele or even Sigmund Freud strolling in—a rather select clientele, a concentrate of creative minds the like of which rarely assembled in one place during the twentieth century. This is one of the cutlery designs that set the tone for the century.

△ This simple *Oval Tray*, designed by Josef Hoffmann in 1923 and produced by us in four sizes (2003), may be considered the epitome of the myriad tray made in contemporary industry.

◁ A brief comment on the unusual shape of the bowl and of the tablespoon. In the original design, the bowl was set transversely to the handle, a very fetching solution ideal for sipping consommés, but not very practical for vegetable soups, or broths with pasta or rice. Together with Elisabeth Schmuttermeier, the curator at MAK, who helped us in our critical reconstruction, we made the decision to manufacture not just the original version but also a more contemporary—for want of a better word—version with a bowl coaxial to the handle.

▷ Designed in 1938 and unveiled (in silver) at the 1940 Triennale, the *Caccia* cutlery range was considered a splendid design example of "Lombard classicism" and was praised by Gio Ponti due to the masterful balance struck between the craft past and the industrial future of household objects.

Luigi Caccia Dominioni, Livio & Pier Giacomo Castiglioni

◁ Thanks to an agreement with Castiglioni heirs, this cutlery is now reproduced in silver plated nickel-silver and in steel (1990): Luigi Caccia Dominioni himself oversaw completion of the series, designing the items missing from the original project fifty years later.

ALESSI

The Alessi Museum

museo
alessi

○ Our role as a "Factory of Italian Design," somewhere between manufacturing and art, has gradually attracted the attention of museums of applied arts and industrial design from all over the world, and there have been many exhibitions of our work. Thanks to our constant experimentation over the years, we have produced a vast and fascinating body of prototypes which, together with our historical output and countless objects collected over the decades from all over the globe, form a valuable cross-section of the history of our field and our aims. The Alessi Museum, opened in spring 1998, has been built to house all the objects, designs, images and documents of all types regarding the history of Alessi and, more generally, the history of household articles. This new museum has come into being within our own structure; it is destined to reinforce our metaproject outlook and production policy (through the support of historical authorities), as well as provide a more direct and comprehensive channel for communicating with the museums we have been working with for some time. Designed by Mendini and curated by Francesca Appiani, the Alessi Museum is open to researchers, scholars, journalists and students. The Alessi Museum can be visited by appointment.

△ Setting up an Alessi Museum is a physiological evolution in a two-decade-long process of theme and solution development. Many of the publications that have come out over this period presaged this outcome, if nothing else for the intrinsic, captivating poetic and artistic riches of this wealth of projects, for the density of intellectual debate from which they have emerged. Nevertheless, the Museum has opened its doors at a unique time, in a climate where the very function of museums is at a crossroads. The Museum is part of a phenomenon that is spontaneous and curious: Alessi is taking on the age/nature/identity of a museum, a novel kind of museum.

▽ Set up in a building inside the Crusinallo factory complex, the museum displays a huge number of prototypes, products no longer in production, graphics, blueprints and prints covering the history of Alessi. Also, engravings, designer installations, historic photos, books, magazines and catalogues. It is a veritable specialist museum of twentieth-century applied art and design, with a number of very rare exhibits; what's more, it also serves as an ordered archive of Alessi's cultural identity.

ALESSI

▷ In March 2002 the Alessi Museum, in collaboration with Modena's Galleria Civica, presented the travelling show "Fotografia e Design. L'immagine Alessi" (Photography and Design. The Alessi Image), a path of eighty pictures offering a new slant on the theme of the relationship between the photographic image and the design object.
The images were selected from a total of over thirty thousand kept in the photographic archives of the Alessi Museum and are the work of several of the most famous photographers in the field of design and advertising, from Aldo Ballo to Gianni Berengo Gardin, Santi Caleca to Studio Azzurro, Stefan Kirchner to Jean Baptiste Mondino.

△ Alessandro Mendini has designed installations for various Alessi exhibitions: right, the polymorphous organism for the exhibition "Not in production – Next to Production," held in Milan in 1988 and in Ghent in 1990. Hans Hollein designed the display for the *Tea & Coffee Piazza* project (above, left) with the now famous split arch, as well as the major "Paesaggio casalingo" exhibition, presenting Alessi's output from 1921 to 1980, opening at the Milan Triennale in December 1979, then travelling to Linz and Berlin in 1980.

▽ The Alessi Museum is a founder member of the Museimpresa association, established in 2001, and embracing Italian company museums, architecture and archives.

MUSEIMPRESA

▽ Pictures of Alessi exhibitions in Caracas, Sydney, Paris, and Tel Aviv recall the many shows held in museums all over the world: "Tea & Coffee Piazza" (United States, Milan, Krefeld, Zurich, Aachen, Barcelona, Kyoto, Ghent, Antwerp 1983–86); "La Conica e altre caffettiere" (Milan 1983); "Tafelarchitektur" (Rotterdam, Düsseldorf 1985); "Création" (Lyon 1986); "La caffettiera e Pulcinella" (Milan 1987); "L'atelier Alessi" (Paris, Brussels, Scandinavia, Brazil, Zagreb 1989–95); "100% Make Up" (Florence, Ghent, Groningen, Roanne, Nice 1992–93); "Alessi 1921–1994" (France 1994); "Manger (Vevey 1994); "For the sake of use" (Tel Aviv 1994); "F.F.F." (Ljubljana 1995); "Achille Castiglioni Designer" (Barcelona-Milan-Bergamo-Weil am Rhein-New York-Tokyo-Niitsu-Breda 1995–98); "Starckologie" (Frankfurt, Paris 1996); "Metallarbeiten" (Berlin 1996); "Omaggio ad Aldo Rossi" (Milan-Hamburg 1998); "Alessi" (New York 1998); "Alessi, The Dream Factory" (Caracas 1998), "Life with Alessi Design. Italian Wind to Colour Japanese Life" (Tokyo 2000).

▽ During the summer of 2001 a group of young architects, guided by Riccardo Dalisi, organized the exhibition project "Viaggio dall'idea all'oggetto. I prototipi del Museo Alessi" (a journey from an idea to a project. Alessi Museum's prototypes). Held in the Dorica room at Naples Palazzo Reale, the exhibition explained the development and experimentation – usually not well known – that leads to the creation of a product.

▽ "La Fabbrica dei Sogni. Alessi dal 1921" (The Dream Factory. Alessi since 1921) has become a travelling exhibition, where the company's history is told by means of unknown prototypes, designs and materials kept in the Alessi Museum.

SUMMER FESTIVAL

▷ The Alessi Summer Festival was held in 1999 at the Forum in Omegna. The main event was the "Show of shows, twenty years of Alessi exhibitions," curated by the Atelier Mendini and Bruno Gregori. It comprised an anthology of the most significant moments from the many Alessi exhibitions over the years, providing an unusual glimpse of design utopias and trends, as well as indicating future directions of development.

◁ Year 2000: Mendini's *Merry-go-round of Wonders* at the Kunst- und Ausstellungshalle der Bundesrepublik Deutschland in Bonn was our way of taking up the invitation by Michael Erlhoof to feature in a major exhibition he was curating, comparing design in Germany and Italy during the second half of the twentieth century. The exhibition went under a soccer-inspired title "4-3," bringing up memories of a match that Italians are pleased to remember.

The Wonder Shops

○ As I have tried to convey in this book, our "dream factory" has, in the last eighty years, produced a catalogue of objects of a richness and complexity that is perhaps without equal in our industry: over 100 designers, more than 2,000 items, non-stop development of new projects, taking in a range of materials which, starting with our roots in metals, has gradually expanded to include plastics, wood, crystal, porcelain, appliances and consumer electronics.

The large number of objects, not to mention the multitude of object types and different design approaches, means that extra special care is required in presenting them to the public. In the last few years it has become increasingly clear that as well as the many multi-brand stores around the world, it was a good idea to have exclusive Alessi stores, offering the best possible presentation and display of our wares. In 1997 I asked Atelier Mendini to develop a blueprint for "an ideal Alessi store." The fundamental concept was to handle Alessi objects as if they were fairy-tale characters, each with its own story and traits, and a desire to transmit joy and aesthetic energy. The interior design of these stores, which we have created in a number of cities around the world, combines the excitement of fairy tales with the effects of a *underkammer*, the "Wonder Chamber" popular during the Renaissance and Baroque. These display locations have been devised

△ The Barcelona *Flagship* (Josef Castells), in Mallorca 251.

▽ The hallmark of the Mendini-designed Berlin *Flagship* (2000, Alessio Alessi), located in the Stilwerk building in Kantstrasse 17—Mendini was also responsible for the Düsseldorf Flagship on the next page —is the important decorative motif in precious Bisazza mosaic tesserae, an Italian homage to the architectural renaissance of the German capital.

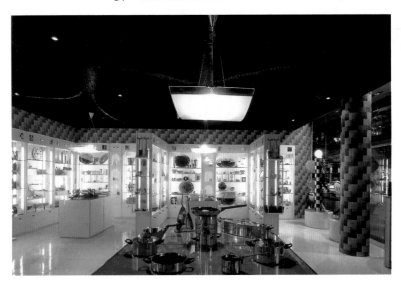

to summarize the characters produced by the "dream factory," and to transmit the customer a sense of adventure in design and the homescape. Spring 2002 sees Alessi *Flagships* in Milan (Enrico Corti, Corso Matteotti, 9), Hamburg, Berlin, Düsseldorf, Stockholm, Oslo, Helsinki, Singapore (Lim Choon Hong, Penang 9), Tokyo, Atlanta (Scott Reilly, 805 Peachtree Street), Los Angeles

△ The Düsseldorf *Flagship* (2000, Alessio Alessi), at 15 Grünstrasse.

◁ The San Francisco *Flagship* (Cat Morrison and Carol Bale Malcom), in 424 Sutter Street.

▽ Following on from his Milan store, the Hamburg *Flagship* (1996, Marcus Rexter), located in the Stilwerk building, looking out onto the Baltic at 68 Grosse Elbstrasse, was our second store to be built along the lines of this new concept. The fact that Alessi has three *Flagships* in Germany is a sign of our attention towards this nation, which is the world's largest design market.

(Philippe Rousselin, 8801 Beverly Bl.) and London. We have adhered to the same display concept for the shops-within-shops we are setting up in many of the world's finest multi-brand stores—at present there are around 103 of them.

ALESSI

▷ *Flagships* in Helsinki at 39 Fredrikinkatu (1998, Mikael and Anita Ruola), Oslo at 6 Skovveien (1998, Tom Howard), and Stockholm at 20 Humlegardsgatan (1995, John Baroi). They represent Alessi's embassies to Scandinavia, a region that is particularly discerning when it comes to good design.

▽ London, 22 Brook Street: a small Victorian building is the six-storey home to the UK first Alessi *Flagship* and the Alessi UK offices (2000, Jan Vingerhoets).

◁ For the Tokyo Alessi Building (1999, Shigeto Mutoh) in Kita-Aoyama Minatoku, the first project encompassing an entire (diminutive as it may be) urban building, the Atelier Mendini worked with a similar DNA to the Crusinallo factory's, establishing a kinship to span the continents.

Collaboration with Other Companies

○ The end of the nineties marks Alessi's last evolution (for the time being). Our "dream factory" has become a research laboratory in the field of applied arts which in the last quarter of the twentieth century, working with the leading talents of international design, successfully brought together poetry, creativity, culture, vision, sincerity, modernity and design excellence like no other industrial organisation in the world. Our very nature has led us to become involved in production contexts that, because of their technological specificity but also the different type of distribution, could never have become direct fields of operation for Alessi S.p.A. As a result, we decided to offer our skills in design management and our vision of design as an overall creative discipline to companies working with products that are far removed from our original one. These are highly specialised companies in their technological and distribution fields that, in our opinion, with our help could create truly new items conceived for the evolved public of the twenty-first century. Items characterised by that mix of eccentricity and style, playfulness and culture, irony and elegance that is distinctive mark of Alessi items: a game of opposites for which I think no other brand can flaunt such convincing assistance and such a specific vocation.

Il Bagno Alessi

◁ The first operation was the most complex and ambitious. We joined forces with three European companies, complementary to each other, representing the finest tradition in the field of bathroom fixtures. Under the design direction of Stefano Giovannoni we developed a complete scenario for the bathroom area: from ceramic fixtures to faucets and fittings, accessories, mirrors, furniture, shower stalls, lighting and bathroom fabrics.

The *Alessi Bathroom* was presented to the public in the spring of 2002.
It's easy to imagine that this complex operation (its coordination sorely tested the steady nerves of our design manager Massimo Bortott) involved the collaboration of a large number of people at the various companies. The photograph by Giuseppe Pino on the previous page, symbolically succinct due to space requirements, portray only one person for each partner: in addition to Stefano and me—we're easy to recognise—we have Donata Fantoni from the Italian Inda, Luis Sabanès from the Swiss Laufen and Pekka Paasikivi from the Finnish Oras. All dressed up strictly with elements from the fabrics designed by Elisa Giovannoni for the *Alessi Bathroom*.

Alessi Watches

▷ The second operation (2002) revolves around
the theme of *Wristwatches*, and it was developed
in collaboration with SII Marketing International Inc.
of Austin, Texas (on the Alessi side, I was assisted
by Kristiina Lassus and Silvano Guglielmazzi),
a company that combines vast professional experience
in the American and Japanese watch-making field.
Working with them, we perfected the new Alessi
watches designed for a public that can orient itself
critically in the consumer society—a public I like
to imagine with the metaphor of the dreamer,
the person who can use his or her imagination
and is thus capable of appreciating the poetics and
the singular union of eccentricity and style that makes
our items unique.

From top to bottom, watches by Achille Castiglioni,
(yes, it's his historic project designed for us together
with Max Huber in 1988—finally rediscovered!), Ron
Arad, two by Stefano Pirovano, Piero Lissoni and Stefano
Pirovano again.

Monographs

E. Sottsass, *Esercizio formale*, exhibition catalogue, Alessi, Crusinallo 1979.

A. Mendini, *Paesaggio casalingo. La produzione Alessi nell'industria dei casalinghi dal 1921 al 1980* (1st ed. Domus, Milan 1979), Internationales Design Zentrum, Berlin 1981.

F. Burkhardt, *Cibi e riti–Essen und Ritual*, proceedings of the design seminar held at the IDZ in Berlin in January 1981, Alessi, Crusinallo 1982 (1988²).

Var. Authors, *Tea & Coffee Piazza*, with introduction by Alessandro Mendini, Shakespeare & Company, Milan 1983 (1986⁵).

A. Rossi, *"La conica", "La cupola" e altre caffettiere*, Alessi, Crusinallo 1984 (1988³).

Var. Authors, *Staedelschule*, Alessi, Crusinallo 1985.

E. Medagliani and F. Gosetti, *Pastario ovvero atlante delle paste alimentari italiane*, Alessi, Crusinallo 1985.

P. Scarzella, *Il bel metallo. Storia dei casalinghi nobili Alessi*, Arcadia, Milan 1985.

A. Alessi and A. Gozzi, *La cintura di Orione. Storia, tecnica e uso dei recipienti da cottura in metallo per la Grande Cucina*, Longanesi, Milan 1987.

R. Dalisi, *La caffettiera e Pulcinella. Ricerca sulla caffettiera napoletana 1979–1987*, Alessi, Crusinallo 1987 (1989²).

P. Scarzella, *Steel & Style. The Story of Alessi Household Ware*, Arcadia, Milan 1987.

A. Alessi, *Not in Production / Next to Production*, exhibition catalogue, Alessi, Crusinallo 1988.

A. Alessi and A. Gozzi, *La cucina Alessi*, Econ, Dusseldorf 1988.

L. Polinoro, *L'officina Alessi. Alberto Alessi e Alessandro Mendini: dieci anni di progetti, 1980–1990*, F.A.O./Alessi, Crusinallo 1989.

Var. Authors, *Philippe Starck*, F.A.O., Crusinallo 1990.

Var. Authors, *Christopher Dresser*, F.A.O., Crusinallo 1991.

Var. Authors, *Rebus sic…*, Centro Studi Alessi (ed.), con interventi di A. Alessi, F. La Cecla, L. Leonini, M. Migliari, M. Pandolfi, L. Polinoro, L. Scaraffia, L. Vercelloni, F.A.O./Alessi, Crusinallo 1991.

A. Branzi, *Il dolce stil novo (della casa)*, F.A.O./Alessi, Crusinallo 1991.

R. Dalisi, *L'oggetto eroticomiko*, P. Scarzella (ed.), F.A.O./Alessi, Crusinallo 1991.

A. Mendini, *La fabbrica estetica*, F.A.O./Alessi, Crusinallo 1992.

Le fabbriche del design italiano. Alessi: une dynastie d'objets, exhibition catalogue, Istituto Italiano di Cultura di Parigi, Carte Segrete, Rome 1993.

L. Polinoro, *Family Follows Fiction*, F.A.O., Crusinallo 1993.

Var. Authors, *Alessi. The Design Factory*, Academy Editions, London 1994.

R. Poletti, *La cucina elettrica. I piccoli elettrodomestici da cucina dalle origini agli anni settanta*, Electa/Alessi, Milan 1994.

E. Mari, *Ecolo*, F.A.O., Crusinallo 1995.

B. Pedretti, *Opere postume progettate in vita. Metallwerkstatt Bauhaus anni '20–anni '90*, Electa/Alessi, Milan 1995.

Var. Authors, *L'oggetto dell'equilibrio*, Electa/Alessi, Milan 1996.

M. Meneguzzo, *Philippe Starck distordre*, Electa/Alessi, Milan 1996.

G. Bertsch, *Der Wasserkessel von Michael Graves*, Verlag Form, Frankfurt 1997.

F. Burkhardt, J. Capella and F. Picchi, *Perché un libro su Enzo Mari*, Federico Motta Editore, Milan 1997.

S. Gronert, *Die Espressokanne von Richard Sapper*, Verlag Form, Frankfurt 1997.

Alessi. The Design Factory, Academy Editions, London 1998².

F. Sweet, *Alessi Art and Poetry*, Thames & Hudson, London 1998.

M. Collins, *Alessi*, Carlton Books Limited, London 1999.

M. Collins, *Alessi*, Bassermann, Niedernhausen 1999.

A. Alessi, *La fabbrica dei sogni*, Electa, Milan 2000.

Selected Bibliography

XI Triennale, exhibition catalogue (Milan, Triennale), Milan 1957.

XV Triennale, exhibition catalogue (Milan, Triennale), Milan 1973.

A. Pansera, *Storia e cronaca della Triennale*, Longanesi, Milan 1978.

Design & Design, exhibition catalogue of the XIth Compasso d'oro, ADI, Milan 1979.

XVI Triennale, exhibition catalogue (Milan, Triennale 1979–1982), Alinari, Florence.

Var. Authors, *Design ist unsichtbar*, exhibition catalogue, Löcker Verlag, Vienna 1980.

Centrokappa, *Il design italiano negli anni '50*, Domus, Milan 1980.

A. Grassi and A. Pansera, *Atlante del design italiano 1940–1980*, Fabbri, Milan 1980.

Bio 9, Bienale Industrijskega Oblikovanja, exhibition catalogue, Bio, Ljubljana 1981.

XII Compasso d'oro, exhibition catalogue, Electa, Milan 1981.

Var. Authors, *Conseguenze impreviste–Arte, moda, design*, exhibition catalogue (Florence), Electa, Milan 1982, vol. III.

Var. Authors, *Gli anni trenta. Arte e cultura italiana*, exhibition catalogue, Mazzotta, Milan 1982.

Var. Authors, *Nuove intenzioni del design*, R.D.E., Milan 1982.

P. Arnell, T. Bickford and K. Vogel Wheeler, *Michael Graves. Buildings and Projects 1966–1981*, Rizzoli International, New York 1982.

V. Gregotti, *Il disegno nel prodotto industriale. Italia 1960*. Var. Authors, *1980*, Electa, Milan 1982.

F. Irace, *Precursors of Post Modernism–Milan 1920–30's*, exhibition catalogue, The Architectural League, New York 1982.

Italian Re-Evolution, exhibition catalogue (La Jolla Museum of Contemporary Art), Milan 1982.

Provokationen–Design aus Italien. Ein Mythos geht neue Wege, exhibition catalogue (Hannover, Deutscher Werkbund), Hannover 1982.

Dal cucchiaio alla città nell'itinerario di 100 designer, exhibition catalogue, Electa, Milan 1983.

Design, exhibition catalogue (Zurich, Kunstgewerbe-Museum), Zurich 1983.

Design since 1945, exhibition catalogue (Philadelphia, Museum of Art), Rizzoli International, New York 1983.

Icsid design Milano, exhibition catalogue, R.D.E., Milan 1983, vol. IV.

C. Mann, *Clotet – Tusquets*, Gustavo Gili, Barcelona 1983.

Var. Authors, *L'economia italiana tra le due guerre 1919–1939*, exhibition catalogue, Ipsoa, Rome 1984.

Bio 10, Bienale Industrijskega Oblikovanja, exhibition catalogue, Bio, Ljubljana 1984.

Castiglioni A. Meister des Design der Gegenwart, exhibition catalogue, Electa, Milan 1984.

Memphis Design, Kruithuis, s'Hertogebosch 1984.

Tre anni di design, XIII Compasso d'oro, exhibition catalogue, R.D.E., Milan 1984.

P. Arnell and T. Bickford, *Aldo Rossi. Buildings and Projects*, Rizzoli International, New York 1985.

A. Bangert, *Italienisches Möbeldesign. Klassiker von 1945 bis 1985*, Modernes Design, Munich 1985.

S. Bayley, *The Conran Dictionary of Design*, Conran Octopus, London 1985.

Dalla tartaruga all'arcobaleno, exhibition catalogue, (Milan, Triennale), Triennale–Electa, Milan 1985.

H. Hollein, *Hans Hollein*, exhibition catalogue, A+U Publishing, Tokyo 1985.

S. Kohmoto, *Contemporary Landscape. From the Horizon of Post Modern Design*, exhibition catalogue (Kyoto, The National Museum of Modern Art), Kyoto 1985.

K. Sato, *Alchimia, Never Ending Italian Design*, Rikuyo-sha, Tokyo 1985.

Strategie d'intesa, exhibition catalogue, Electa, Milan 1985.

H. Wichmann, *Die neue Sammlung. Ein neuer Museumstyp des 20. Jahrhunderts*, exhibition catalogue, Prestel, Munich 1985.

Var. Authors, *Les carnets du design. Les arts de la table*, Mad-Cap, Paris 1986.

A Table, exhibition catalogue (Paris, Centre Georges Pompidou), Paris 1986.

Bio 11, Bienale Industrijskega Oblikovanja, exhibition catalogue, Bio, Ljubljana 1986.

Caravelles. L'enjeu de l'objet, exhibition catalogue, Grenoble–Lyon–Saint-Etienne 1986.

A. Grassi and A. Pansera, *L'Italia del design. Trent'anni di dibattito*, Marietti, Casale Monferrato 1986.

R. Krause, V. Pasca and I. Vercelloni, *La mossa del cavallo. Mobili e oggetti oltre il design*, Condé Nast, Milan 1986.

Österreichische Galerie – Wien, *Cleto Munari Collection. Silver and Architects*, Vienna 1986, pp. 26–29.

Teyssot, Il progetto domestico. La casa dell'uomo: archetipi e prototipi, exhibition catalogue (Milan, XVII Triennale), Electa, Milan 1986.

Var. Authors, *The Post Modern Object*, exhibition catalogue, Ga Pindar, London 1987.

J. Capella and Q. Larrea, *Diseño de Arquitectos en los '80*, Gustavo Gili, Barcelona 1987.

M. Collins, *Towards Post-Modernism: Design since 1985*, British Museum Publications, London 1987.

Hans Hollein. Metaphores et metamorphoses, exhibition catalogue (Paris, Centre Georges Pompidou),

Paris 1987.

S. von Moos, *Venturi Rauch & Scott Brown*, Rizzoli International, New York 1987.

B. Munari, M. Bellin and A. Branzi, *Descendants of Leonardo da Vinci. The Italian Design*, Graphic-Sha, Tokyo 1987.

Nouvelles tendences. Les avant-gardes de la fin du XXe siècle, exhibition catalogue (Paris, Centre Georges Pompidou), Paris 1987.

XIV Premio Compasso d'oro, exhibition catalogue, Silvia, Milan 1987.

A. Rossi, *Aldo Rossi Architect*, Electa, Milan 1987.

Var. Authors, *Alessandro Mendini*, exhibition catalogue (Groningen, Groninger Museum), Giancarlo Politi, Milan 1988.

Var. Authors, *Design und Wohnen*, exhibition catalogue, Helga Treft Verlag, Frankfurt 1988.

Var. Authors, *Sottsass Associates*, Rizzoli International, New York 1988.

Bio 12, Bienale Indusrijskega Oblikovanja, exhibition catalogue, Bio, Ljubljana 1988.

G. Bosoni and F.G. Confalonieri, *Paesaggio del design italiano 1972–1988*, Edizioni di Comunità, Milan 1988.

C. Colin, *Design d'aujourd'hui*, Flammarion, Paris 1988.

Id., *Starck*, Pierre Mardaga Editeur, Liège 1988.

Der Verzeichnete Prometheus, exhibition catalogue, Nishen Verlag, Berlin 1988.

Design in Catalogna, exhibition catalogue, BCD, Barcelona 1988.

F. Fischer, *Design Heute*, exhibition catalogue (Frankfurt, Deutsches Architekturmuseum), Frankfurt 1988.

C. Gambardella, *Il progetto leggero. Riccardo Dalisi: vent'anni di design*, Clean, Naples 1988.

F. Haks, *Alessandro Mendini Sketsboek–Sketches*, Froukje Hoekstra, Amsterdam 1988.

B. Klesse, *Hundert Jahre Museum für Angewandte Kunst der Gegenwart. Mäzenatentum*, exhibition catalogue (Cologne, Museum für Angewandte Kunst), Cologne 1988.

La caffettiera napoletana e Pulcinella, exhibition catalogue (Taranto, Circolo Italsider), Editrice Scorpione, Taranto 1988.

Richard Sapper. 40 Progetti di Design 1958–1988, exhibition catalogue, Arti Grafiche Mazzucchelli, Milan 1988.

R. Sambonet, *L'arte in tavola*, Industria Grafica Ronda, Milan 1988.

P. Sparke, *Italienisches Design*, Thames and Hudson, London 1988.

H. Wichmann, *Italian Design 1945 bis heute*, Die Neue Sammlung, Munich 1988.

Var. Authors, *Alessandro Mendini*, exhibition catalogue, Giancarlo Politi, Milan 1989.

Var. Authors, *From Matt Black to Memphis and Back Again*, Blueprint/Wordsearch, London 1989.

M. Collins and A. Papadakis, *Post-Modern Design*, Rizzoli International, New York 1989.

P. and R. Colombari, *Effetto acciaio*, exhibition catalogue, Arti Grafiche Giacone, Turin 1989.

Compasso d'oro. Italian design, exhibition catalogue, Silvia Editore, Milan 1989.

G. Lueg, *Design*, exhibition catalogue (Cologne, Museum für Angewandte Kunst), Cologne 1989.

L. Peel, P. Powell and A. Garrett, *An Introduction to 20th Century Architecture*, Quinted Publishing, London 1989.

XV Premio Compasso d'oro, exhibition catalogue, Silvia Editrice, Milan 1989.

Var. Authors, *Michael Graves. Buildings and Projects, 1982–1989*, Princeton Architectural Press, Princeton 1990.

A. Bangert and K.M. Armer, *Design der 80er Jahre*, Bangert Verlag, Munich 1990.

N. Bellati, *New Italian Design*, Rizzoli International, New York 1990.

J. Capella and Q. Larrea, *Oscar Tusquets objets dans le parc*, exhibition catalogue, Gustavo Gili, Barcelona 1990.

Collezione per un modello di museo del disegno industriale italiano, exhibition catalogue, Fabbri, Milan 1990.

L. Gobbi, F. Morace, R. Brognara and F. Valente, *I Boom*, Lupetti & Co., Milan 1990.

Metall für den Gaumen, exhibition catalogue, beim Herausgeber, Vienna 1990.

J. Myerson and S. Katz, *Kitchenware*, Conran Octopus, London 1990.

Var. Authors, *Aldo Rossi Architecture 1981–1991*, Princeton Architectural Press, Princeton 1991.

Var. Authors, *New and Notable Product Design*, Rockport Publishers, Rockport 1991.

O. Boissiere, *Starck*, Taschen Verlag, Cologne 1991.

J. Capella and Q. Larrea, *Nuevo diseño español*, Gustavo Gili, Barcelona 1991.

S. Casciani and G. Di Pietrantonio, *Design in Italia 1950–1990*, Giancarlo Politi, Milan 1991.

2e Quadriennale internationale de design, exhibition catalogue, Caravelles 2, Lyon 1991.

P. Dormer, *The Illustrated Dictionary of Twentieth Century Designers*, Quarto Publishing, London 1991.

Formes des metropoles–Nouveaux designs en Europe, exhibition catalogue (Paris, Centre Georges Pompidou), Paris 1991.

P. Polato, *Il modello nel design*, Hoepli, Milan 1991.

Primavera del disseny. Barcelona 1991 spring design, exhibition catalogue (Barcelona, Ajuntament de Barcelona), Barcelona 1991.

Var. Authors, *Objects and Images*, U.I.A.H., Helsinki 1992.

Casa Barcelona, exhibition catalogue, IMPI, Barcelona 1992.

A. Ferlenga, *Aldo Rossi architetture 1988–1992*, Electa, Milan 1992.

Nuovo bel design, exhibition catalogue, Electa, Milan 1992.

Starck in Wien, exhibition catalogue, Die Kommode, Vienna 1992.

M.C. Tommasini and M. Pancera, *Il design italiano*, Mondadori, Milan 1992.

U. Brandes, *Richard Sapper*, Steidi, Göttingen 1993.

B. Fitoussi, *Objects affectifs*, Hazan, Paris 1993.

Cristina Morozzi, Massimo Morozzi, L'Archivolto, Milan 1993.

Design und Wohnen 2, exhibition catalogue, Helga Treft Verlag, Frankfurt 1993.

P. Dormer, *Design since 1945*, Thames and Hudson, London 1993.

H. Höger, *Ettore Sottsass Jun.*, Ernst Wasmuth, Berlin 1993.

La fabbrica estetica, exhibition catalogue, ICE, Milan 1993.

Museum für Angewandte Kunst. Ein Wegweiser von A bis Z, Cologne 1993.

S. Prinz, *Besteck des 20. Jahrhunderts*, Klinkhardt & Biermann, Munich 1993.

Richard Sapper Design, exhibition catalogue (Cologne, Museum für Angewandte Kunst), Cologne 1993.

M. Turinetto, *Dizionario del design*, Lupetti & C., Milan 1993.

Var. Authors, *Atelier Mendini. Una utopia visiva*, Fabbri, Milan 1994.

Arts et formes ou 40 variations pour une histoire d'eau, exhibition catalogue (Paris, Musée du Louvre), Paris 1994.

M. Byars, *The Design Encyclopedia*, Laurence King, London 1994.

F. Burkhardt, *Marco Zanuso*, Federico Motta, Milan 1994.

Raymond Guidot, histoire du design 1940, Hazan, Paris 1994.

Totocchio, exhibition catalogue, F & T Boo, Vicenza 1994.

A la Castiglione, exhibition catalogue, Istituto Italiano di Cultura, Barcelona 1995.

XVII Premio Compasso d'oro, exhibition catalogue, Silvia Editrice, Milan 1995.

A. Pansera, *Dizionario del design italiano*, Cantini, Milan 1995.

Pour un couteau. design et couverts 1970–1990, exhibition catalogue, Thiers 1995.

Thomas Haufe. Design, Dumont, Cologne 1995.

Var. Authors, *Design im Wandel*, Bangert Verlag, Bremen 1996.

Var. Authors, *Dictionnaire international des arts appliques et du design*, Editions du Regard, Paris 1996.

Alessandro Mendini 30 colours, V+K Publishing, Bussum 1996.

A. Branzi, *Il design italiano 1964–1990*, exhibition catalogue, Electa, Milan 1996.

S. Casciani, *The Art Factory*, exhibition catalogue, Editrice Abitare Segesta, Milan 1996.

F. Haks, *Mendini*, L'Archivolto, Milan 1996.

P. Starck, *Vanity Case*, Taschen, Cologne 1996.

Werkzeuge. Design des Elementaren, Landesgalerie, Austria 1996.

Bella forma, Landschaftsverband Westfalen-Lippe, Hagen 1997.

E. Biffi Gentili, *Cleto Munari. Dandy Design*, Electa, Naples 1997, p. 113.

F. Burkhardt and C. Morozzi, *Andrea Branzi*, Dis Voir, Paris 1997.

S. Delialis, *Thessaloniki Design Museum*, Thessaloniki Design Museum, Thessaloniki 1997, p. 23.

M. Eidelberg (ed.), *Design for Delight. Alternative Aspects of Twentieth-century Decorative Arts*, Montreal Museum of Decorative Arts - Flammarion, Paris-New York 1997, pp. 62, 82, 128, 130.

Gout design, Musée de Louviers, Paris 1997.

S. Gronert, *The 9090 Cafetiere by Richard Sapper*, Verlag Form, Frankfurt 1997.

M. Fortis, *Il made in Italy*, Il Mulino, Bologna 1998, pp. 110, 111, 112, 113.

Industridesign Igår og Idag, Henie Onstad Kunstsenter, 1998.

C. Morozzi, *Oggetti risorti*, Costa & Nolan, Milan 1998.

J. Carmel-Arthur, *Philippe Starck*, Carlton, London 1999.

A. Ferlenga (ed.), *Aldo Rossi. Tutte le opere*, Electa, Milan 1999, pp. 216–219.

Futur Compost. El diseño en Barcelona para el proximo siglo, Institut de Cultura de Barcelona/Electa, Barcelona 1999.

Museum voor Sierkunst en Vormgeving, *Grande Vaso di Gent opera di Andrea Branzi*, Museum voor Sierkunst en Vormgeving, Gent 1999, p. 27.

C. Neumann, *Design in Italia*, Rizzoli, Milan 1999.

A. Scevola, S. San Pietro, *Prodotto industriale italiano contemporaneo*, L'Archivolto, Milan 1999.

The Israel Museum, Jerusalem, *Design and Architecture at the Israel Museum. Portrait of a Department. 1973–1997*, Israel Museum, Jerusalem 1999, pp. 74, 123, 137.

Abitare il Tempo. *Laboratori metaprogettuali*, Verona Fiere, Verona 2000, p. 24.

ADI Associazione per il disegno Industriale, *1998–1999 Design Index*, Editrice Compositori, Bologna 2000, pp. 143, 145, 156.

S. Delialis, *Design routes*, Thessaloniki Design Museum, Thessaloniki 2000, pp. 18, 33, 35–36, 38.

Design: 4 : 3. 50 Jahre italianisches & deutsches Design, Kunst-und Ausstellunghshalle der Bundesrepublik Deutschland, Bonn 2000, pp. 208–211.

C. and P. Fiell, *Design del XX secolo*, Taschen, Cologne 2000.

Kunst Halle Krems, *Haltbar bis… immer schneller. Design auf Zeit*, Dumont, Cologne 2000, pp. 10, 14, 43.

Istituto Italiano di Cultura di Varsavia, Triennale di Milano, Instytut Wzornictwa Przemystowego, *1945–1990. 100 oggetti del design italiano*, Warsaw 2000, pp. 19, 52, 63, 68, 71.

C. Lloyd Morgan, *20th Century Design: a Reader's Guide*, Architectural Press, Oxford 2000.

Louisiana Museum of Modern Art, *Vision and Reality*, in "Louisiana Review," vol. 41, no. 1, Humlebaek 2000, p. 88.

Moderna Museet Projekt, Gäst Hos, Hinrich Sachs, *Anna Gili, designer*, Stockholm 2000, pp. 8, 10.

National Gallery of Australia, *Techno Craft. The Work of Susan Cohn 1980–2000*, National Gallery of Australia, Canberra 2000.

Nuages, *Milton Glaser opere 1960-2000*, Nuages, Milan 2000, p. 85.

M. Romanelli (ed.), *Aperto Vetro 2000. Architetti e designer a confronto con il vetro quotidiano*, Electa, Milan 2000, pp. 83, 136, 196.

C. Taverna, A. Rauch, *Milton Glaser*, Venice 2000, p. 85.

Young Nordic Design. The generation X, Design Forum Finland, 2000.

P. Antonelli, *Workspheres. Design and Contemporary Works Styles*, The Museum of Modern Art, New York 2001, pp. 177, 185.

Bienal Internacional de Arte de Vila Nova de Cerveira, XI Bienal, Cerveira 2001, pp. 38–39.

A. Branzi (edited by), *Italia e Giappone: design come stile di vita*, Tokyo, Nihon Keizai Shimbun Inc, 2001, pp. 17, 23, 40–41, 62–63, 65–66, 83, 142, 225, 309.

D.B. Brownlee, D.G. De Long, and K.B. Hiesinger, *Out of the Ordinary. Robert Venturi, Denise Scott Brown and Associates. Architecture, Urbanism, Design*, Philadelphia Museum of Art, Philadelphia 2001, pp. 222–224, 232–237.

L. Dal Bò, M. La Guidara (ed. by), *Sicilia Europa: prospettive del nuovo design*, Bruno Leopardi Editore, Palermo 2001, pp. 52, 58–59, 82.

R. Fayet (ed.), *70s versus 80s. Möbel-Glas-Keramik*, Arnoldsche Art Publishers, Zurich 2001, pp. 123, 125.

Italia Giappone 2001, Design supermarket. Stefano Giovannoni, Nava Press, Milan 2001, pp. 8, 13–19, 26–31, 40–49, 54–57, 60, 70–72.

La Triennale di Milano, *1945-2000. Il design in Italia, 100 oggetti della Collezione Permanente del Design Italiano La Triennale di Milano*, Gangemi Editore, Rome 2001, pp. 38, 97, 113, 126, 130, 148.

Università degli Studi "Federico di Napoli", Scuola di Specializzazione in Disegno Industriale, *Bricchi, caraffe, caffettiere. Viaggio dall'idea all'oggetto*, Paparo Edizioni, Naples 2001 (the book presents the exhibition "Viaggio dall'idea all'oggetto.")

S. Annicchiarico (ed.), *Animal house. Quando gli oggetti hanno forme e nomi di animali*, Edizioni della Triennale, Milan 2002, pp. 64–65, 67, 83, 98–99, 103–106.

S. Annicchiarico (ed.), *Il mondo in una stanza. Quando gli oggetti hanno nomi di luoghi*, Edizioni della Triennale, Milan 2002, pp. 50–51, 63, 70, 72–73, 88–89, 96, 100–101.

S. Annicchiarico (ed.), *Non sono una signora. Quando gli oggetti hanno un nome di donna*, Edizioni della Triennale, Milan 2002, pp. 25, 43, 70, 84, 100–101.

Christoper Dresser and Japan, Insho-sha, Japan 2002, pp. 20–21.

Fondation Cartier pour l'art contemporain, *Alessandro Mendini, Vincent Beaurin, Fabrice Domercq. Fragilisme 2002*, Fondation Cartier pour l'art contemporain, Paris 2002, pp. 26, 54, 101.

J. Kipnis, A. Massie, *Mood River*, Wexner Center for the Arts, Columbus (Ohio) 2002, pp. 67, 69.

Satyendra Pakhalé Cultural Nomad. From Projects to Products. Dal Progetto al Prodotto, Editoriale Modo, Milan 2002.

M. Senaldi, *Permesso di soggiorno. Il design senza fissa dimora*, Galleria Luisa Delle Piane, Milan 2002, pp. 26, 28.

*Alessi Objects in Museum Collections
and Public Institutions*

Photograph Credits

Stedelijk Museum, Amsterdam; Museo de Artes Decorativas, Barcelona; Bauhaus-Archiv, Museum für Gestaltung, Berlin; Kunstgewerbemuseum SMPK, Berlin; National Gallery of Australia, Canberra; The Denver Art Museum, Denver; Kunstmuseum Düsseldorf, Düsseldorf; Museum Folkwang, Essen; Museum für Kunsthandwerk, Frankfurt; Museum voor Sierkunst, Gand; Design and Applied Art (Mudesa), Garabaer (Islanda); Israel Museum, Jerusalem; Groninger Museum, Groningen; Museum of Applied Arts, Helsinki; Louisiana Museum of Modern Art, Humlebaek; Kunstgewerbemuseum, Cologne; Museum für Angewandte Kunst, Cologne; The National Museum of Modern Art, Kyoto; Centro Cultural de Belém, Lisbon; Bio Design Collection, Ljubljana; Victoria and Albert Museum, London; National Gallery of Victoria, Melbourne; Triennale di Milan, Milan; The Minneapolis Institute of Arts, Minneapolis; Die Neue Sammlung, Staatliches Museum für Angewandte Kunst, Munich; Yale University Art Gallery, New Haven; The Brooklyn Museum, New York; The Metropolitan Museum of Art, New York; The Museum of Modern Art, New York; Ostfriesisches Tee-Museum, Norden; Henie Instad Art Center Kunstsenterhovikodden, Norway; Museum of Applied Art, Oslo; Musées des Arts Décoratifs, Paris; Philadelphia Museum of Art, Philadelphia; Museum Boymans-van-Beuningen, Rotterdam; Museu de Arte, São Paolo; Deutsches Klingenmuseum, Solingen; Powerhouse Museum, Sydney; MAK Österreichisches Museum für Angewandte Kunst, Vienna; Kunstgewerbemuseum der Stadt Zurich, Zurich ; Museum für Gestaltung, Zurich.

Alessi Archives, Atelier Mendini Archives, Andrea Branzi Archives, Riccardo Dalisi Archives, Eurostand Archives, Florence Gift Mart Archives, Stefano Giovannoni Archives, Michael Graves Archives, Sottsass Associati Archives, Guido Venturini Archives, Arici and Bernardi, Aldo and Marirosa Ballo, Maria Vittoria Backhaus, Simone Barberis, Bauhaus Archiv, Raffaello Benedetti Bra, Giovanni Berengo Gardin, Bergamo and Basso, Riccardo Bianchi, Luigi Brenna, Santi Caleca, Franco Capra, Attilio Del Comune, Ramak Fazel, Alberto Ferrero, Fotorama, Enzo Franza, Giacomo Giannini, Pino Guidolotti, J. King, Stefan Kirchner, Mattew Klein, Carlo Lavatori, Lucio Lazzara, Salvatore Licitra, Bruno Marchetti, Mauro Masera, Jean-Baptiste Mondino, Occhiomagico, Carlo Paggiarino, Sergio Pancaldi, Giuseppe Pino, Valerio Rebecchi, Franco Sargiani, Renato Sartori, Oliver Schuh and Barbara Burg, Luciano Soave, Studio Azzurro, Top Studio of Zappalà, Leo Torri, Oliviero Toscani, Emilio Tremolada, Franco Uberti, Tom Vack, Walter Zerla. Illustrazioni di Libero Gozzini and Wilma Incerti, Jordi Labanda, Studio Softroom, Suresh Sethi, Tiger Tateishi.

Holders of rights to any unidentified photographs sources should contact the publisher.

This book was printed by Mondadori Electa S.p.A.
at Mondadori Printing S.p.A., Verona, in the year 2003